Loyalist Echoes of 1783

Tell My Story Collection

Angeline Gallant

Published by Angeline Gallant, 2022.

LOYALIST ECHOES OF 1783

First edition. July 21, 2022.

ISBN: 979-8231318537

Written by Angeline Gallant.

Table of Contents

"They say you die twice. Once when you stop breathing and the second, a bit later on, when somebody mentions your name for the last time."— *Banksy*

To those whose names are nearly silent—may this be their breath again.

Introduction: Forgotten Lives, Living Stories

They came with seed corn sewn into their hems and infants bundled close. They left behind graves, debt, and soil that would never be theirs. They arrived in strange ports and untamed forests—some with Loyalist patents in hand, others with nothing but faith. And somewhere along the way, their names slipped through the cracks of time.

This is a book about finding them again.

As a genealogist, I've spent years tracing the lives of real men and women who built their homes along the rivers, backroads, and cemeteries of early Canada. These are not the governors or generals history remembers—but their wives, sons, midwives, and schoolmasters. They're the ones who baked the bread, stitched the flags, buried their dead, and kept the diaries that never made it to print.

Each chapter in this volume is dedicated to a historical figure—documented in records, rooted in place, and revived through story. First, you'll meet them as they lived: the dates, locations, marriages, children, and movements that make up their family tree. Then, you'll see them through a creative lens—characters in waiting, rich with fictional potential. Finally, we'll walk where they once stood, with curated travel itineraries that allow you to follow their journey yourself.

This book is for:

The genealogist who longs to humanize their research.

The author looking for grounded inspiration.

The history lover who wants to travel deeper, with purpose and context.

The reader who believes that history is not over—it's just unfinished.

YOU'LL NOTICE MANY of these figures lived through war, migration, poverty, and upheaval. Some of them died young. Some changed their names. Some left behind children who became prominent, others whose stories faded with time. But they all shaped something that remains—and now, they have one more place to live: here.

Welcome to a new kind of heritage book. One rooted in fact. Inspired by fiction. Made for wandering souls who want to remember.

Author's Note

As you begin to read, I invite you to take a step back in time, not just to witness the past, but to feel it. To see the worn faces of those who once walked the land you tread, to imagine their struggles, their hopes, their quiet moments of joy. The names of these people may seem like mere words carved into stones, yet each one holds a story—a history not just of survival but of dreams, loss, and enduring spirit.

In this book, I do not wish to simply present facts and dates. I want to bring these individuals to life in a way that transcends the records and becomes something tangible. A glimpse into the lives of those who were here before us, and who shaped the town we know today.

Genealogy has always been more than names on a chart to me. It's the way I connect to the past, and through it, I find a way to honor the lives of those who came before me. These pages are my way of extending that connection, inviting you to see them—not just as forgotten figures in a history book, but as real people with stories that matter.

This book is also a gift to writers and dreamers. Each profile is more than a historical record—it's a launching point for creativity, a chance to imagine what these people might have thought, felt, or experienced beyond what the facts tell us. Let these stories inspire you, move you, and if you are a writer, may you find a new character to breathe life into. For in the act of remembering, we make them live again.

So, as you walk through Kingston's past, imagine you are there, alongside these souls. Let the streets of 1783 open up to you, and with each step, honor the memory of those who helped lay the foundations of this town. Their stories are your stories, too.

The portraits within these pages are artistic impressions—faces imagined to reflect the life and times of the individuals they accompany. In honoring their memory, my hope is not perfect likeness, but heartfelt tribute.

James Harley

S cene: Spring 1791 – The First to Believe

The spring earth was soft, not yet dry, the scent of pine sap mingling with the sorrow of parting. A small group stood beneath a grey sky in a clearing beside the lake, their coats damp, their hats in hand. The war still smouldered on paper, but for James Harley, it was already over.

Captain Michael Grass knelt beside the grave, a wooden cross resting in his callused hands. His shoulders were stiff, his jaw clenched. But there was grief in his eyes. Harley had not lived to see the town rise, yet here he would rest—in the very soil he believed would hold a future.

"He came north with nothing," Grass said quietly, his voice low and reverent. "Left his home, his kin, his claim to peace. But he came with faith. He believed—before the governors, before the maps were redrawn. He saw it."

No minister had yet been appointed. No church had been raised. And yet, the men bowed their heads as Grass recited the words himself.

"From dust you came, and to this earth you return. Not as a soldier. As a founder."

The others stepped back as the cross was set. The wind off the lake stirred the pine needles, and for a moment, no one spoke.

Grass looked toward the horizon—toward the place he would soon lead others, carrying Harley's memory with him.

"I'll not forget you," he whispered. "And neither will this town."

Years later, St. Paul's Anglican Church would be built above that resting place. The townsfolk would come and go, never knowing that beneath their feet lay the bones of one of the first Loyalists to stake his life on Cataraqui.

But Grass would know. And so would the land.

AUTHOR'S SECTION: WRITING James Harley Into Fiction

Overview:

James Harley died before the final Treaty of Paris was signed, but his faith in the Loyalist settlement at Cataraqui places him among the earliest founders of what would become Kingston. Buried in 1791 beneath what is now St. Paul's Anglican Church, Harley represents the quiet builders—those who committed before there were promises, who saw the future before it had shape.

Writing Tips:

Use Harley as a deeply human figure—faithful, humble, and quietly loyal to both the Crown and his friend, Captain Michael Grass.

He isn't driven by rank or politics but by conviction: he believes in the land and in the vision Grass has for it.

Consider portraying Harley as a settler who supported the Loyalist cause out of duty, but who became truly inspired by the idea of building something new in Upper Canada.

His early death makes him a tragic but powerful symbol—he believed in something he would never see finished.

CHARACTER POSSIBILITIES:

He could be used in flashbacks or recollections by Grass, shaping how Grass views his own leadership.

In a fictional setting, Harley might have recorded his thoughts in a journal, leaving behind words that inspire a younger generation.

His grave beneath St. Paul's could become a place of quiet pilgrimage for descendants or characters seeking meaning.

HISTORICAL CLOTHING & Details:

Picture a well-worn settler's coat, boots thick with clay, and hands callused from cutting timber and hauling stones.

He may have carried a simple weapon—a musket or a hatchet—but he was a builder first.

Likely buried in linen or wool, wrapped with care by his friends, not in uniform but in workman's garb.

THEMES TO EXPLORE:

Sacrifice before certainty: Harley died before any royal approval was granted, making him a symbol of faith over permission.

Friendship and loyalty: His bond with Captain Grass offers an emotional foundation for Grass's own leadership arc.

Buried history: The church above him is both literal and symbolic—faith built upon faith, stones laid over bones. Writers can explore how places remember people even when names fade.

JAMES HARLEY IS NOT the man who led others—but the man who believed first. Every story needs a soul like that: someone who saw the land not as it was, but as it could be. His grave is not just a footnote in Kingston's history. It is its cornerstone.

Let Harley be the whisper in the earth—the first to trust, the first to lie down in peace beneath the soil of a dream.

www.wikitree.com/wiki/Harley-1102[1]

---

1.   http://www.wikitree.com/wiki/Harley-1102

1783

The air over New York held the strange stillness of a city learning how to breathe again. Smoke from hearth fires coiled between the gables of battered buildings, mingling with the sharp tang of sea salt drifting in from the harbor. Ships creaked at anchor, their masts bobbing like weary soldiers at rest. Some bore British flags still, half-furled in defiance or confusion, while others flew no colors at all—uncertain of where their loyalties lay in this new world being born.

The cobblestone streets were pocked and cracked from years of wagon wheels, military boots, and winter frost. Ashes still blackened the foundations of homes burned in earlier riots and occupations. Fences leaned. Signs dangled on rusted hinges. And yet, life pulsed underneath the ruin. Street vendors hawked apples and stale bread. Children chased each other barefoot through alleys once patrolled by Redcoats. A few brave shopkeepers reopened their doors, scrubbing soot from windows and nailing up crude signs that read "Under New Management."

In taverns, voices were hushed and strained. Loyalist families whispered over tankards, contemplating ships bound for Halifax or London. Patriot sympathizers leaned close, murmuring of opportunity and rebirth, of farms to claim and debts to settle. And then there were those who didn't speak at all—free and enslaved alike—watching with keen, haunted eyes as the world reshaped itself without their voice.

Up Broadway, the old Dutch and English buildings stood like tired sentinels, stooped from fire and frost. Overhead, the September sky was pale and hard, the color of pewter, promising another winter. And yet, on the breeze, there was something new—like the distant scent of rain on dry earth. The treaty had been signed. War was over. There would be no more marching feet, no more midnight arrests, no more gallows raised in secret. Not here. Not now.

Still, peace came not as a triumphant shout, but as a long exhale—quiet, unsure, almost fragile.

In the harbor, the last of the British warships floated like ghosts, readying to sail. And as a bald eagle wheeled overhead, someone in the street looked up, smiled grimly, and said, "Well. We kept the damn city after all."

KING'S TOWN, 1783

The First Township

Before it was Kingston, it was King's Town, surveyed in the year of uneasy peace and quiet resettlement—1783—named in loyalty and reverence to King George III by those who had risked everything to remain faithful to Crown and country. Before that, it was simply known as The First Township, a name that felt more like a placeholder than a promise, yet it marked a beginning all the same.

This land at the mouth of the Cataraqui River, where the waters of Lake Ontario opened like a mirror to the sky, bore witness to something ancient long before map lines were drawn. It had been paddled by canoes, hunted on foot, whispered to in Mohawk. But in 1783, its soil was turned by weary Loyalist hands—stone by stone, tree by tree—by soldiers, farmers, widows, and children. Some came by bateaux, others by the ship *Camel*, their past lives folded away like old letters. They arrived with what they could carry, and sometimes, what they could not bear to leave behind.

The settlement was rough, the air sharp, and loyalty no longer guaranteed safety or shelter. But still, they came. From Tryon, Montgomery, Canajoharie, Wyoming, Albany—those names stitched to memory like old prayer beads. They brought with them stories, scars, and a sense of duty that clung to them even in exile.

Here in King's Town, they would plant, build, bury, and begin again. And from these first fragile roots would rise a new kind of country.

Captain Michael Grass

B *orn: February 11, 1735*
    Died: 1813

Born in Roppenheim, Alsace (France), died in Kingston, Upper Canada; Loyalist Leader and Organizer of Kingston Settlement

Scene: November 1783 – The Shores of Cataraqui

The wind coming off the lake smelled of pine and possibility. Captain Michael Grass stood on the rocky edge of the shoreline, his hand resting protectively over the swell of his wife's back as she leaned into him. Anna Margaretha had grown quiet lately, her hands often folded over the roundness of her belly. The baby would come in December. If they could make it through the first snow, they could make it through anything.

Grass gazed toward the woods inland where trees loomed like solemn sentinels. They reminded him of the forests of his childhood in Alsace before his family sailed for the colonies, chasing the promise of land and liberty. How strange to feel the echo of a homeland in this wilderness.

And yet—Cataraqui. He had seen this place before. Years ago, shackled and ragged, he had been held prisoner in the old French fort. Back then it was stone and defiance and the scent of powder in the air. Now the land stretched wide, hushed by snow, but it spoke clearly to him.

"This is the place," he whispered. "We'll build here."

Other Loyalists milled nearby, huddled around tents and carts, chopping wood, unpacking crates. The war had scattered them, turned neighbors into traitors and friends into strangers. But here, in this place—this prison once—he would lay foundations. Not only for a town, but for something larger. For order. For permanence.

The war was over. The Treaty of Paris had seen to that. But the real labor—of rebuilding lives, of anchoring memory to land—was just beginning.

Author's Section: Writing Captain Michael Grass into Fiction

Captain Michael Grass is a gift to historical fiction writers: a man of resolve and vision, with a remarkable backstory that includes being held prisoner at Fort Cataraqui during the French and Indian War—only to return years later as one of the earliest Loyalist leaders to guide settlers there. What was once a place of confinement became the cradle of his legacy.

Born in Roppenheim, Alsace—a German-speaking region of France—Grass brought a unique European sensibility to the New World. He possessed some education, was known for his excellent character, and held fast to a strict personal code of honor. Though he had many chances to enrich himself at the expense of others during the Loyalist resettlement, he refused. He led with conviction, not ambition.

In 1783, he was married to Anna Margaretha Schwartz, his second wife, who was pregnant with their seventh child. Grass believed fiercely in Cataraqui's potential as a settlement site, and in the years to come, he would prove instrumental in the founding of Kingston. He served as a magistrate in its earliest days and performed many of the first marriages. Though raised Lutheran, he worshipped at St. George's Church, where he rented a pew—evidence of his quiet integration into the Anglican fabric of Loyalist society while never forgetting his roots.

Writing Tips:

● **Explore the emotional complexity** of returning to a place of former captivity, now leading families with hope into an uncertain future.

● **Lean into his cultural contrast**—an educated Alsatian German navigating the raw edges of Upper Canada's wilderness.

● **Highlight his moral compass**: opportunities for greed passed him by, and he never reached for them. What kept him honest?

● **Portray him as a family man**: his concern for his pregnant wife and children would have weighed heavily during every decision.

● **Infuse his spirituality**: he saw their exile as a refining fire—God's way of forging a new, upright society from hardship.

Historical Details to Consider:

● Grass may have worn military-style garb with civilian practicality—coarse wool coat, greatcoat, travel-worn boots, perhaps a tricorn or practical felt hat.

● He likely carried ledgers or devotional books in German, documents related to his commission, and personal correspondence.

● His speech may have been colored by Alsatian German phrasing or cadence, giving writers an opportunity to make his voice distinct.

● His daily life would include both civic duties as magistrate and personal tasks settling his own family—giving you texture for scenes both public and intimate.

By writing Michael Grass into your novel, you give breath once more to a man who saw hope where others saw only ruin. He built community from ashes, forged leadership from loss. I've passed you the torch—now let your pages carry it forward.

www.wikitree.com/wiki/Grass-217[1]

Cataraqui United Church Cemetery - Ontario[2]

---

1. http://www.wikitree.com/wiki/Grass-217

2. https://billiongraves.com/cemetery/Cataraqui-United-Church-Cemetery/322918/volunteer

Anna Margaretha Grass (née Schwartz)

S*eptember 25, 1738 – 1816*
Born in Schweigern, Germany; Loyalist Matron, Wife of Captain Michael Grass

Scene: November 1783 – Montreal, Province of Quebec

The city smelled of woodsmoke, snow, and strange tongues. French, English, German, the braying of oxen—Montreal was full of noise, but inside Anna Margaretha's heart, there was only silence.

She sat near the window of the boarding house, hands resting heavily on the swell of her belly. The baby shifted, nudged—another boy, perhaps. Her seventh child, and the coldest birth yet. December loomed, and she would not risk the wilderness of Cataraqui until the child was safely born. Michael had agreed, though she knew it pained him to go ahead without her.

She pressed a folded cloth to her eyes and did not lie to herself about the tears. The Treaty had been signed. The war was over. The British had made peace with their former colonies. But there was no peace inside her—not when peace meant leaving a son behind.

Andreas.

Her firstborn. Her heart's beginning. Born in New York City, when she and Michael still believed the world would settle around them like a homecoming cloak. There had been sickness. So much sickness. She buried him quietly, without even a headstone, in the earth of a city that now belonged to the rebels.

She would never visit him again. Never tend his grave. Never again sit in the Lutheran church on Pearl Street where she once cradled him through sermons, never again light a candle for his soul at Christmas.

The child kicked again. She placed her hand over the spot and whispered to him in German—soft, old words from her village in Schweigern. Words her mother had spoken when she herself was a child, before the ocean, before war, before heartbreak.

"Ruhe jetzt, mein kleiner. Wir fangen neu an."

Rest now, my little one. We begin again.

Author's Section: Writing Anna Margaretha Grass into Fiction

Anna Margaretha Schwartz Grass is a quiet heroine—a woman of endurance, of memory, and of deep faith. Born in Schweigern, Germany, she immigrated to the American colonies and married Captain Michael Grass, becoming his second wife. By 1783, she was pregnant with their seventh child and preparing to give birth in Montreal while her husband helped lead the Loyalist settlement of Cataraqui (Kingston).

She and her family were Lutherans. In New York, they had attended the Lutheran church faithfully—likely Trinity Lutheran Church on Pearl Street, one of the few established congregations at the time. This faith was a pillar in her life, especially in grief. Her first child, Andreas, had been baptized and buried in that city. The grave she would never see again.

Writing Tips:

- Use Anna's motherhood and faith as central themes: she is defined by what she loves and what she's lost.

- Let her voice reflect the quiet depth of a woman who has endured. She is not bitter—she is rooted, like the liturgy she once heard weekly in German.

• Consider her cultural identity as a German Lutheran immigrant. These traditions shaped her food, her language, her views on duty, family, and community.

• You might imagine her as someone who sings hymns under her breath when no one is listening. Her faith is a private strength.

• Explore her sorrow for Andreas—not as a dramatic moment, but a thread that lingers in small, reverent acts: folding baby clothes, lighting candles, whispering prayers.

Historical Details to Consider:

• She would have worn modest, practical garments: a wool gown, apron, perhaps a fichu tucked into her bodice and a linen cap or kerchief. German Lutheran women often dressed simply, with neatness valued above fashion.

• She may have carried a small Lutheran prayer book in German or kept a woven cloth from her homeland.

• Food and home rituals would have centered around Old World German traditions: simple soups, braised meats, and braided loaves on holy days.

Bringing Anna Margaretha to life means giving voice to the thousands of Loyalist women who bore war in silence—through loss, labor, and faith. She was never famous. She didn't command men or write proclamations. But she helped build a nation by surviving it. Let your words make her remembered.

www.wikitree.com/wiki/Schwartz-2742[1]

---

1.   http://www.wikitree.com/wiki/Schwartz-2742

Eva Margaretha Grass

Juli 9, 1763 – May 16, 1858*
    *Born in New York City, New York Colony; Died in Kingston,
Ontario, Canada*

Scene: Autumn 1783 – Montreal

Eva stood by the hearth, her hands folded in the stiff fabric of her apron. The air in the rented house was damp with rain and boiled cabbage. Outside, the wind rattled the shutters like bones.

Her mother sat quietly in a chair near the window, swollen with child, eyes swollen too. Papa was gone again—off in meetings with other Loyalists, men with hard faces and harsher choices. The war was over, they said. A treaty had been signed in Paris. King George had made peace with the rebels. But none of them felt peace. Not yet.

Eva pressed her lips together and glanced toward the folded letter on the table—the one from her father. She had already read it three times.

They would not be returning to New York.

They were going to Cataraqui. The place where her father had once been a prisoner, back in the old war with the French. Now he called it a new beginning. He spoke of land and promise, of leading other Loyalist families there to start again. Her older brother Andreas was buried in New York soil, but they would never be able to visit him. She did not say this aloud. She had learned, already at twenty, how to carry grief without breaking apart.

Eva crossed the room, picked up the letter, and read it again. She could hear her father's voice in the words—careful, formal, but full of conviction. He believed in Cataraqui. He believed in duty. She knew, deep down, that he needed to believe it for all their sakes.

Her mother groaned slightly and shifted in the chair. The baby would come in December. It would be born in Montreal—another city, another chapter. The whole world was shifting beneath their feet like cracked ice.

Eva stepped to the window and touched the cold glass.

She didn't know what this new place would be like. She only knew that when her father turned toward the frontier, she would not let him walk into it without her.

Author's Section: Writing Eva Margaretha Grass into Fiction

Eva Margaretha Grass was born in New York City in 1763 and would go on to live a full and long life in Kingston, Ontario, passing away in 1858. As the second-born child of Captain Michael Grass and Anna Margaretha Schwartz, she would have been twenty years old at the time of the Treaty of Paris and her family's migration to Upper Canada.

While women like Eva often appear only in birth and death records, they lived rich, complex lives. Her survival into the mid-19th century means she witnessed Kingston's transformation from a Loyalist outpost to a thriving city—and perhaps carried in her memory the smell of salt from the harbor of New York and the sound of her father's boots walking away toward duty.

Writing Tips:

- Write her with quiet strength. At twenty, Eva was likely helping her pregnant mother, managing younger siblings, and coping with enormous emotional upheaval. She was old enough to feel the finality of leaving New York and young enough to still dream of love and belonging in a new land.

- Explore her loyalty to family, particularly her parents. Michael Grass was not just a father but a respected Loyalist leader—Eva may have felt torn between admiration and fear for what lay ahead.

● Eva may be seen as a keeper of family memory. She likely passed stories of New York and the Loyalist exodus down to her own children and grandchildren.

Clothing and Setting:

● As a young woman in 1783, Eva would likely have worn a simple linen shift, stays, a wool petticoat, and a fitted jacket or bedgown. Modest, working-class attire, but with care given to neatness.

● Hair would have been pinned up, perhaps under a linen cap or kerchief, with little adornment beyond what was practical.

● Consider scenes where she sews, cooks, or tends a fire—acts of domestic strength during a time of upheaval.

Character Themes to Consider:

● Displacement and memory: the feeling of losing home but forging a new one.

● A daughter's perspective on loyalty, faith, and courage.

● The quiet fortitude of Loyalist women, who carried both grief and survival into the next generation.

Eva lived through revolution, resettlement, and rebirth. Now, authors can give her voice—carry her across the page with the dignity she earned and the spirit she passed on.

www.wikitree.com/wiki/Gress-226[1]

1. http://www.wikitree.com/wiki/Gress-226

John Michael Grass

October 4, 1765 – January 18, 1849
Born in New York City, New York Colony; Died in Kingston, Ontario, Canada

Scene: Autumn 1783 – Montreal

John Michael sat on the steps of the house, carving absently at a strip of wood with his penknife. Each curl of bark fell like a thought he didn't know how to say aloud. The street smelled of horses and wet leaves. Somewhere, a baby cried. Somewhere else, a soldier laughed too loud. The world was trying to find its new shape. He wasn't sure he liked it.

Seventeen years old. Old enough to understand that nothing was simple. Old enough to hear the word "peace" and know that it didn't mean safety.

His father had gathered them the night before with a letter in his hand and purpose in his voice. They were leaving Montreal. Going to a place most people couldn't pronounce—Cataraqui. The name still sounded strange in John's mouth. He tried whispering it now under his breath.

He remembered New York. The stone streets, the church bells, the books. He remembered walking behind his father through Lutheran pews with candle smoke curling toward the ceiling. He remembered the smell of his older brother Andreas—leather and ink—and the way his mother stopped speaking his name after they left him behind in the city graveyard.

John swallowed hard.

He knew he'd never see that grave again. That was the price. That was what it meant to stay loyal to the Crown.

He wanted to be brave like his father. He wanted to make something of the wilderness they were headed into. But just for now, for one more moment, he let himself be seventeen—stuck between what was and what would be.

He ran his thumb along the edge of the wood he was carving. Tomorrow, he'd rise early and pack what was left. The road west waited for them.

And he would follow his father into the new world, because that's what a son did.

Author's Section: Writing John Michael Grass into Fiction

John Michael Grass was born in 1765, the third child of Captain Michael Grass and Anna Margaretha Schwartz. Just shy of adulthood when the war ended, John Michael would have been old enough to feel the sting of displacement and the weight of inheritance. His name appears in the records not as a soldier or officer, but as a son of a founding Loyalist family—one of the young men who would become the bedrock of early Kingston society.

He lived until 1849, spanning a lifetime that saw Upper Canada rise from untamed frontier to structured colony.

Writing Tips:

• He is a perfect figure to explore coming-of-age themes during upheaval. As a teenager in exile, he's at a crossroads—wanting to follow in his father's Loyalist footsteps, yet shaped by loss, uncertainty, and the hard wilderness ahead.

• He may wrestle with questions of identity. What does it mean to be a Loyalist when the Empire has abandoned its people to start over in the cold woods of Upper Canada?

• Write him with layered emotions: the grief of leaving his brother Andreas behind, the admiration for his father's leadership, the silent strength of a young man growing into his name.

Clothing and Context:

• As a Loyalist youth in 1783, John would have worn practical clothing: linen shirts, a wool coat or waistcoat, breeches, and possibly hand-me-down boots or patched shoes.

• Authors might portray him working alongside his father, clearing brush, surveying land, or helping his mother prepare for the birth of another sibling.

• He likely had basic schooling and could read or write, especially given his father's leadership role and church attendance.

Character Themes to Explore:

• Loyalty and legacy: the role of a son continuing his father's mission.

• Coming of age in exile: how a teenager might internalize displacement and duty.

• Faith and silence: the Lutheran background of the Grass family offers a path for introspection, guilt, and hope.

Let authors take John Michael Grass and breathe into him all the depth he deserves. Let them shape him into a young man who saw war not only on battlefields but in the ache of leaving behind everything familiar. He was not just a name on a record—he was part of the first generation born under one flag, then raised under another.

Now it's time to tell his story.

www.wikitree.com/wiki/Grass-434[1]

---

1. http://www.wikitree.com/wiki/Grass-434

Peter Grass

January 27, 1770 – June 25, 1855
Born in New York City, New York Colony; Died in Kingston, Canada West

---

Scene: Autumn 1783 – News of the Peace

The grown-ups cried when the news came.

Peter didn't understand why.

The war was over. Wasn't that what they'd been waiting for? No more redcoats marching, no more whispered news at the table, no more watching the worry in his mother's eyes when his father stayed out too long.

But the peace didn't bring joy. Not for them.

He sat outside the tent they'd pitched along the river, the wind pulling through the trees, and listened to the muted voices from within. His father's voice low and heavy. His mother's—thick with tears.

Peter had heard the word "Paris" before. That's where it ended, they said. Where men in powdered wigs had signed a paper to declare that everything was settled. But no one had asked the Grass family if they were ready for it to end.

The war may have ended on paper, but for people like them, it only meant one thing: they were never going back.

He clutched the stick he'd been carving. His fingers were cold. So was the ground beneath him. It wasn't like New York here. There were no carriages, no markets. Just the endless forest and the sound of a distant loon.

They couldn't even say goodbye to Andreas. Peter hadn't known his older brother well—he had died when Peter was just a baby—but they always visited his grave. His mother always brought flowers. Now there would be no more visits. The peace treaty had closed a door they couldn't open again.

Peter understood something in that moment. The war hadn't just stolen lives. It had stolen *place*. His family had no country now, not really. Just a patch of wilderness and a name on a Loyalist list.

But then he looked up at his father—Captain Grass—standing in the clearing with his arms crossed, surveying the land like he had already decided it would belong to them. And something settled in Peter's chest.

Maybe this was where they would belong next.

Author's Section: Writing Peter Grass into Fiction

At thirteen, Peter Grass was just old enough to be aware of the weight of history unfolding around him, but still young enough to process it through the eyes of someone longing for belonging. He was part of the first generation raised entirely within the Loyalist exile—and eventually, the Canadian project.

Writing Tips:

● Use Peter to explore the complexities of inherited loyalty. He didn't fight, but he bears the consequences of his parents' choices and the Empire's fall.

● His reactions to the war's end should blend confusion, loss, and the slow birth of resilience. He doesn't fully grasp the politics, but he feels the rupture.

● As an adult, Peter may reflect back on this moment as the day he understood what it meant to be a Loyalist—not by bloodshed, but by displacement.

Clothing & Details:

• Peter would have worn practical hand-me-downs: a linen shirt, breeches, stockings, a wool coat or short jacket, and perhaps a knit cap. His shoes may have been worn or ill-fitting from the journey north.

• He likely spoke both English and some German, with Lutheran teachings grounding his worldview.

Character Arcs to Explore:

• *Belonging and displacement*: What does it mean to build a new home when you're told you've lost the old one forever?

• *Youth and awakening*: The Treaty of Paris was signed by men far away, but it changed the course of Peter's entire life.

• *Legacy and roots*: Peter lived long enough to see Kingston become a capital. Writers can explore how that moment shaped the man he became.

You've been given the framework—now it's your turn. Let Peter speak through your stories. Give him thoughts, feelings, questions, hopes. Let your pen walk him through the wild woods of 1783 into the Canada he helped build.

www.wikitree.com/wiki/Gress-227[1]

---

1.   http://www.wikitree.com/wiki/Gress-227

Daniel Grass

D*ecember 23, 1773 – after 1804*
Born in Schenectady, New York Colony

Scene: Autumn 1783 – When Grown-Ups Whisper

Daniel was only nine years old when the peace was declared.

He didn't really know what peace meant—only that his older siblings stopped playing, his mother cried more often, and his father spoke in hushed, clipped German when he thought the children were asleep. Daniel pretended not to listen. But he always listened.

From where he sat in the wagon, feet swinging, he could see the trees thinning ahead, the curve of the river glinting in the sunlight. The adults spoke of a place called "Cataraqui," like it was both a promise and a test. His father—who had once been a prisoner there—seemed to treat it like a final chapter. But Daniel wondered if maybe it was a beginning.

The word "peace" had fallen from the mouths of the soldiers like something sacred. But to Daniel, it felt strange. It meant they wouldn't be going back to New York. It meant the house he barely remembered in Schenectady was lost. It meant Andreas would stay buried in that place forever, far from his mother's reach.

Daniel pressed his face against the side of the wagon, watching the wild country roll past. The grown-ups called it wilderness. He thought it looked like a place where you could build forts and climb trees and maybe never have to wear shoes.

They said the king had lost. Or maybe it was the king who had let them down. Daniel didn't understand all of it, but he knew this: things were changing. And no one, not even Papa, could pretend that home meant what it used to.

Still, when his father lifted him from the wagon and set him down on the cold earth, Daniel looked out over the clearing with a quiet resolve.

If this was where they had to live now, he would make it his kingdom.

Author's Section: Writing Daniel Grass into Fiction

Daniel Grass represents a bridge between generations—the Loyalists who remembered the colonies and the children who would come to call Upper Canada home. He was born in the waning years of war and raised during the uncertain founding of a new world.

Writing Tips:

- Capture Daniel's youth without making him naive. Children during this era matured quickly, especially during wartime.

- Use sensory details to shape his experience: the rough roads, the tension in adult voices, the unfamiliar Canadian wilderness.

- Let Daniel's innocence contrast with the exhaustion of his older siblings and the burdens of his parents.

Clothing & Details:

- As a younger child, Daniel would have worn a linen shirt, short breeches, knitted stockings, and possibly a homespun wool coat. His shoes may have been hand-me-downs.

● Being raised in a Lutheran household, he would have been familiar with Scripture readings, prayers, and hymns in German and English.

● Like his siblings, Daniel likely spoke a mix of English and German.

Character Arcs to Explore:

● *Coming of age in exile*: What does it mean to grow up with no memory of "home," only stories?

● *Adapting vs. remembering*: Would Daniel embrace the new land or yearn to understand what was lost?

● *Survivor's bond*: He lived past 1804. What did he carry from those early Loyalist years into adulthood?

Daniel is a vessel for resilience, for childlike curiosity shaped by adult sorrow. His voice is soft but enduring. Now it's your turn to let him grow up again—on your pages. Let him run barefoot through your chapters, his eyes wide, asking the questions his parents never could.

www.wikitree.com/wiki/Gress-228[1]

---

1. http://www.wikitree.com/wiki/Gress-228

Mary Grass

O*ctober 1776 – November 16, 1816*
Born in Tryon County, New York Colony

Scene: Autumn 1783 – A Girl Between Worlds

Mary wasn't sure what peace looked like.

The word had drifted through camp like a breath of warm air through canvas—*The war is over.* But she couldn't remember a time when the world hadn't been shaped by her father's boots, her mother's quiet prayers, and the restlessness of one move after another.

Seven years old, the sixth child of Michael and Anna Margaretha Grass, Mary had always lived in the shadow of war. She had been born as the colonies split in two, when lines of loyalty cracked even families apart. Now, those lines had hardened into borders.

Her older siblings spoke in hushed tones when they thought she wasn't listening. Words like *Cataraqui* and *evacuation* stirred in her ears like foreign magic. She didn't understand everything—but she understood what it meant when her mother looked longingly at a folded piece of paper, her fingers trembling. That paper marked a grave in New York. The name was Andreas. A brother Mary had never met.

She wouldn't get to meet him either.

Mary watched her mother sew slowly, belly round with her seventh child, each stitch laced with sorrow and steel. Her father had decided. They would follow the others north, to a place he once called a prison—Cataraqui, now a promised land for the Loyalists.

Mary would miss the familiar corners of their cramped quarters in New York. She'd miss the songs sung in German during evening prayers, the bustle of the Lutheran church where everyone knew her family by name. But she didn't say any of that out loud.

Instead, she helped where she could—fetching water, folding linen, trying not to feel too small when her father mentioned the British ships and the journey ahead. There were no younger siblings to mind, no one to care for but herself. Still, she stood straighter, listened more carefully, and imagined what her father saw in the wilderness. Hope, maybe. A home.

When they boarded the boat, Mary turned once to look back. Not at the skyline or the buildings or even the church. She looked toward the invisible place where Andreas rested, her feet planted firmly on the deck and her hand clenched around the wooden rail.

She didn't cry. She would save that for another time. Right now, she needed to be brave.

Author's Section: Writing Mary Grass into Fiction

Mary Grass stands at the threshold of peace and wilderness. Born in 1776 at the height of political chaos, she was a child of war—but not of battle. Her life offers the rare lens of a Loyalist daughter whose memories are forged not in muskets or politics, but in the quiet shifts of family sacrifice, forced migration, and enduring faith.

Writing Tips:

- Explore Mary as someone precocious and observant. Children at that age were often far more responsible than modern readers may expect.

- Her inner world could be rich with imagination, shaped by hymns, family stories, and unspoken grief.

- Use subtle contrasts: her childlike wonder versus the weary strength of her parents, especially her mother.

Clothing & Historical Details:

- At seven, Mary would've worn a linen shift with a simple woolen petticoat and bodice or shortgown. A linen cap or kerchief was typical for modesty.

- She likely walked barefoot in warm months and wore hand-me-down shoes in colder weather.

- The family spoke German at home and attended a Lutheran church in New York, where music, scripture, and discipline shaped her early worldview.

Themes & Character Arcs:

- *Coming of age during upheaval*: Show Mary's gradual understanding of what it means to leave behind a grave, a home, a name.

- *The promise of a new life*: What does a wilderness settlement look like to a girl raised among the crowded streets of New York?

- *Legacy and loss*: Mary's story is anchored by what she never knew—her brother Andreas, the land they left, the country they once called home.

Through Mary, readers can experience the Loyalist journey from a child's view—an intimate window into displacement, identity, and the endurance of hope. She is a quiet yet powerful thread in the Grass family tapestry, and now she is yours to bring to life.
www.wikitree.com/wiki/Gress-229[1]

---

1.   http://www.wikitree.com/wiki/Gress-229

Beneath the Barracks Flags: The Martial Pulse of Kingston

The ground trembled beneath the measured tread of boots.

From the limestone heights of Fort Frontenac to the marshy edges where the Cataraqui met Lake Ontario, Kingston pulsed with the cadence of military life. Frost bit at canvas and leather, and morning drills stirred flocks of blackbirds from the trees. Smoke curled from chimneys and campfires alike, mingling with the shouts of officers and the steady thud of hammers reinforcing stockades and shelters.

This was no mere outpost—it was a depot, a hub, a garrisoned heart beating at the edge of a still-fractured continent.

Scarlet and green jackets moved in purposeful lines. The 5th Regiment's veterans, weathered from old campaigns, drilled beside the younger men of the 100th. The Queen's Rangers, lean and cunning, patrolled the perimeter with the quiet confidence of men who'd fought in forests before. The Royal Canadian Volunteers struck a proud profile—sons of this soil proving loyalty with steel. The 41st and 60th brought with them the discipline of Europe, their banners rippling in the northern wind as musket barrels caught the pale sunlight.

Within Kingston's registers—worn volumes inked by clerks who barely looked up from their work—these regiments are named with little fanfare. But in the mud, in the snow, in the sound of hooves and the grind of supply wagons, their presence was anything but forgettable.

Kingston did not simply host soldiers—it made them. It tested their endurance, forged their friendships, and held their ghosts.

They came with orders. Some left with scars. Others stayed, married, died, and were buried beneath the rising churches and parade squares they once helped guard.

This was not yet a country, but it would become one—and here, among uniforms and cannon smoke, was where its backbone began to form.

Corporal's Honour: Men Who Carried the King's Cause Beyond the Battlefield

Introduction:

The war officially ended with pen and parchment—the Treaty of Paris, signed in September 1783. But for the men who had shouldered muskets in His Majesty's name, peace did not mean rest. There were no parades, no homecomings. Only the long retreat north, away from lands that no longer welcomed them.

These corporals, often overlooked by history, bore the quiet burden of loyalty. They had led men through snow and ash, and now they led their families across rivers and into dense northern forests. They were the backbone of Loyalist settlement: disciplined, dependable, and often destitute.

Their war did not end when the cannons fell silent. It continued in the slow, grueling work of starting over in a raw land with frozen fingers and hungry children. They fled not as defeated soldiers, but as exiles with purpose—determined to plant order and allegiance in soil that had never known either.

Here are their names. Their ranks. Their sacrifice.

Corporal Forrester

D. 1783 – Buried in the Upper Burial Ground, Kingston, Upper Canada

A Loyal Soldier, Laid to Rest in the Land He Helped Secure

Scene: Late Autumn, 1783 – Corporal Forrester Hears the War is Over

The campfire snapped gently, throwing sparks into the brittle autumn air. Corporal Forrester stood apart from the others near the edge of the clearing, his breath rising in thin puffs as he stared toward the northern sky. His back ached. His hands were stiff. But his spine was straight, his boots polished with the stubbornness only a Loyalist soldier could muster.

In his hand was a tattered broadsheet, delivered hours ago by a courier from Quebec: the war was over. Officially, finally, irrevocably over.

He folded the paper without reading it twice. He didn't need to. His war had ended long before the ink dried.

"So that's it," he muttered. "No trial. No reckoning. Just... peace."

Behind him, settlers murmured—families who had lost farms, sons, homes. Some wept. Some drank. Some stared at the fire in silence. And there, near the edge of the camp, stood Michael Grass, speaking quietly with a group of men about Cataraqui.

Forrester watched him a moment, then nodded to himself.

"Let the governors send us east," he scoffed softly. "They don't know the land. Don't know what we bled for. But Grass—he does."

He drew a breath, the wind slicing through his worn coat, and clenched the treaty paper in his fist. "If we must begin again, better to follow a man who stood with us when the world turned upside down. He's earned that."

A young boy ran past, chasing a dog through the frost. Forrester watched the child vanish into the trees and felt something stir in his chest. Not bitterness. Not rage. Something gentler. Something that surprised him.

Hope.

He looked north. Toward Cataraqui. Toward the wilderness that might yet become a town.

"Maybe I'll not live to see the steeple rise or the streets laid straight," he murmured. "But the earth will remember us. The stone will rest above our bones. And maybe one day, someone will walk these roads and know we were here."

He turned back toward the fire, his figure swallowed by the dusk, and walked slowly into the warmth of the Loyalist camp.

He would live to see the snow fall once more, to help carve a path toward the place they would one day call Kingston. And when his time came, the earth would take him quietly—buried beneath what would become the Upper Burial Ground. And later, as if history wished to lay its own benediction, the great stone walls of St. Paul's Anglican would rise above his resting place.

A church atop a soldier's bones. A fitting memorial for a quiet watchman of the Crown.

AUTHOR'S SECTION: WRITING Corporal Forrester at War's End

Overview:

Corporal Forrester embodies the weary resilience of the Loyalist rank-and-file. He isn't looking for vengeance or applause—only a place to build, and a reason to believe it was all worth it. His reaction to the official end of the war is complex: relief, reflection, and an unshakable loyalty to those like Michael Grass, who earned his respect through action, not title.

Writing Tips:

Let Forrester be the steady voice amid chaos. He isn't loud, but he carries weight.

He doesn't mourn the end of the war—but he feels the cost. Let that come through in gestures: a folded paper, a distant look, a callused hand over the heart.

His faith in Grass offers a subtle way to show how loyalty can shift from monarchs to men of principle.

CHARACTER POSSIBILITIES:

He can serve as a mentor, grandfather figure, or steadying presence to younger characters.

His burial under what becomes St. Paul's Church makes him a literal and symbolic foundation of Kingston—he fits beautifully in flashbacks, ghostly recollections, or sacred memory.

CLOTHING AND DETAILS:

Late-war British or Provincial uniform, threadbare and patched.

A simple wedding ring (perhaps widowed), a small carved pipe, a keepsake from home.

Perhaps a faded ribbon, worn in memory of a lost child or wife.

Frostbite, stiffness, a hand he can no longer close fully—signs of a soldier's wear.

THEMES TO EXPLORE:

Legacy: Forrester doesn't seek monuments—but he hopes to be remembered, even if only in stone.

Obedience vs. Leadership: His loyalty to Grass—not just the Crown—opens the door for discussing what it meant to follow men instead of governments.

The Unseen Cost: His death is quiet, but it echoes—writers can return to it in future volumes, or in the foundations of the new town.

FORRESTER ISN'T JUST a soldier. He's the man who laid his bones into the land so others could build over them. In that, he becomes more than a character—he becomes Kingston's first whisper.

Let him speak.

www.wikitree.com/wiki/Forrester-2536[1]

---

1.   http://www.wikitree.com/wiki/Forrester-2536

Corporal Forbes

D. 1783 – Buried in the Upper Burial Ground, Kingston (later beneath St. Paul's Anglican Church)
A Loyalist Who Walked Into the Wilderness and Lay Down Among the Foundations

Scene: Late Fall, 1783 – On the March to Cataraqui

They said the war was over. The words rang out like bells through the Loyalist camps—*peace.* Some wept. Some cheered. Others, like Corporal Forbes, merely nodded.

His face was leathery with age and weather, his back hunched slightly under years of burden. The corporal's uniform hung a little loose now, worn thin from time and hardship. His boots were patched, his hands calloused and shaking, but his spine still straightened when Captain Grass spoke.

He had made his choice months before: to follow the Captain north into the wilderness, to help establish something new for those who had remained loyal to the Crown. He'd packed light. What little he owned he carried, and what little he loved had long since been taken by war.

But now, as they prepared to cross into Cataraqui, the official word came: *The Treaty of Paris has been signed.*

James knelt in the frost, scooping up a handful of the brittle soil. He let the cold earth run through his fingers. "It's finished," he murmured. "God help us—it's finally finished."

He looked up as others cheered, and his lips formed a faint, crooked smile. But the weight in his chest didn't lift.

He wasn't a young man anymore. He felt it in his bones. He had made it this far—across the battlefield, through retreat, hunger, and bitter loyalties tested by fire. And now, at the threshold of a new land, he knew he would not live to see it thrive.

But he would see it begin.

He leaned on his musket and turned to the younger men. "You remember this day," he said, voice gravelly but clear. "The war may be over, but what you build next will matter more. You fight for peace now."

He was buried within the year—beneath the earth he had claimed as his last act of faith. And later, over his grave, a church was raised—St. Paul's Anglican, its walls unknowingly cradling the bones of a man who had believed in the future.

Author's Section: Writing Corporal Forbes Into Fiction

Corporal Forbes is a powerful character for writers who want to explore the passage between worlds—the old order dying and a new land rising from its ashes. He represents the Loyalist soldier who saw war's end not as triumph, but as transition.

How to Use Him in Fiction:

- He can be a steadying force to younger settlers or soldiers, his calm born from sorrow and lived wisdom.

- His death shortly after arriving at Cataraqui offers authors a poignant reminder that not everyone who helped found Kingston lived to enjoy it.

- He might share a moment of quiet conversation with Captain Grass, or offer a blessing to those he knows will carry the work forward.

What He May Have Worn:

- A threadbare Loyalist uniform—likely patched, stained, and faded from years of wear.

- A simple cravat and waistcoat, with practical outerwear suited for cold marches.

- Possibly a tricorne hat or forage cap, depending on what he retained from his service.

- A powder horn and musket, more ceremonial now than practical.

Themes to Explore:

- *The passing of generations:* Forbes bridges the old world and the new.

- *Faith and sacrifice:* His grave beneath the church becomes both literal and symbolic.

- *The cost of loyalty:* He loses much, but never betrays his cause.

Torch for Authors: Through Corporal Forbes, you can show that even unnamed, overlooked lives held deep meaning. His grave may be long forgotten beneath Kingston's streets, but his story—and the stories of thousands like him—deserve to be retold, reimagined, and remembered.

www.wikitree.com/wiki/Forbes-7702[1]

---

1.   http://www.wikitree.com/wiki/Forbes-7702

Colonel William Johnson

"Ashes and Ice"

Kingston, Upper Canada – November 1783

The lake was already crusting over when Corporal William Johnson stepped off the shallop and onto the raw, frozen bank. Ice cracked underfoot, not thick enough to trust, but eager to make itself known. He shifted his pack higher on his shoulder and let his boots sink into the slush, staring up at the bluff where the first tents and lean-tos of Cataraqui had begun to rise.

Peace, they called it.

He'd heard it from the mouth of the captain back in Sorel, in a voice flat with disbelief: The treaty is signed. It's over. The war is done. But William hadn't felt anything—not joy, not grief, just a strange and hollow quiet, like the one that followed cannon fire.

The war may have ended, but it had spat them out into this—mud, smoke, and timber. The wind off Lake Ontario sliced through his coat, and the stench of wet wool and dampened powder still clung to the others disembarking behind him. They'd left homes in flames. Friends buried in places they'd never see again. Now, this patch of wilderness was meant to be their reward. Their refuge. Their beginning.

He tightened the grip on his musket.

Around him, other Loyalist soldiers shuffled ashore. Some had families waiting with red noses and frightened eyes. Others, like him, arrived alone—men who had lost everything but their duty. In the distance, a Royal Engineer barked orders, trying to make order out of trees and frost. William turned, watching a cart wheel sink halfway into the mire and tip sideways, its load of lumber crashing into the mud with a wet slap.

A man cursed in German. Another laughed bitterly.

William said nothing.

He had fought for the Crown, believing, somehow, that loyalty would buy them security. Justice. Land, maybe. What it had bought was exile. But even that, he thought, might be enough—if only they could build something better here. If only peace was more than paper.

He touched the letter tucked inside his coat. Samuel's handwriting had begun to fade with the damp, but the words lingered sharp: I will arrive late, yes, but not unwilling.

"Come on, Corporal," someone muttered beside him, nudging his arm. "You going to stare at the trees all day or help raise a wall?"

William looked back toward the water, where the boat already drifted away.

"No," he said quietly, setting his jaw as he turned toward the growing camp. "I've had enough of waiting."

And with that, he joined the others in the muck and the wind, hauling timber from the shoreline to the skeleton of a barracks not yet claimed by frost. Peace, maybe. But not rest. Not yet.

For Authors: Giving Voice to Corporal William Johnson

Corporal William Johnson is more than a shadow in a muster roll—he shares blood, if distantly, with the great Sir William Johnson, 1st Baronet, and is therefore a relative of the famed Molly Brant's children. Though no title followed him, nor estate, he carried the surname like a legacy—quietly, steadfastly, and into the mud of Upper Canada.

In 1783, he emigrated to Kingston with the Loyal Rangers, arriving amidst the chaos of a war's aftermath. Though the peace was signed in Paris, men like Johnson understood that peace on paper rarely settled the soul. He stood on Loyalist soil as the trees were felled and the river watched silently—beginning again, far from the land he once called home.

Ways to Bring Him Into Your Novel:

- **As a man caught in legacy's shadow**: You could write him wrestling with his surname, admired or judged by those who remember Sir William. Was he proud? Was he burdened? Did people expect too much—or nothing at all?

- **As a link between worlds**: Use him as a bridge between Loyalist officers and Indigenous allies. Perhaps he carries stories told around Brant family fires, or memories of frontier diplomacy that shaped who he is.

- **As a quiet settler hero**: His journey north could be written as brave, stubborn, or necessary. Let him be the man who builds, not boasts—one who plants for his grandchildren rather than his pride.

Visual Details and Period Tips:

- **Appearance**: He might have resembled his distant kin—dark hair with weathered Anglo-Irish features that he inherited as a descendant from the Johnson line. He would've worn a Loyal Rangers uniform, practical and earth-toned. Picture sturdy boots, a simple sidearm, and a knapsack patched from years on campaign.

- **Post-war Attire**: In Kingston, likely civilian garb with military remnants: homespun coat, wool breeches, a well-worn tricorn or round hat. Maybe he still kept a tobacco pouch from a Brant cousin or a knife gifted in younger days.

- **Speech**: He'd carry a quiet authority. Respectful of rank but not easily awed. His voice could reflect the frontier—direct, seasoned with Mohawk phrases, or references to Albany, Tryon County, and the days before everything changed.

Emotional Anchors to Explore:

- Did William feel torn between his Loyalist ties and Indigenous kin?

- Did he arrive in Kingston with hope or simply because there was no place else to go?

- How did he reckon with what was lost—and what might still be made?

These are the emotional waters he sailed. Your fiction can drop anchor.

Tone Tip: Write William as a man who watches before he speaks. He's not the loudest in the room but the one others follow when they're lost. Use silence and reflection. Let him carry stories passed down from Sir William's campfires—but never claim them loudly.

Closing Torch-Passing: I've traced the lines, followed the fragments. Now I pass the torch. Let this man with a soldier's boots and a diplomat's blood speak again. Tell us what he saw at the edge of empire. Write him into taverns, tents, and timbered cabins. Let him linger in memory, not just in musters.

He may not have worn a baronet's ring—but through your words, let him wear a crown of narrative.

www.wikitree.com/wiki/Johnson-126778[1]

---

1.   http://www.wikitree.com/wiki/Johnson-126778

Colonel Herman Samuel Smith

"The Quiet After" — Corporal Herman Samuel Smith, 1783
Location: Sorel, Quebec – September 1783

The war ended not with a roar, but with silence.

Samuel sat on the stoop of the billet house, one hand curled loosely around a cup of tea gone cold, the other resting on his knee like it belonged to someone else. A grey mist curled over the St. Lawrence, low and thick, clinging to the edge of the earth like smoke from a distant fire. He could barely see the children running by the dock, but he could hear them. Not screaming in fear, not shouting in hunger—just laughing. Real laughter. That had become rare.

A peace had been signed in Paris, they said. He'd heard the words passed around the camp like smuggled sugar, the Treaty this and the King that. Others cheered, even danced. But Samuel had lived long enough to know that war never ended with parchment.

The scars were not on the land alone—they were in the backs of men who limped, in the eyes of those who stared too long at nothing, in the empty places at firesides. He thought of David Mott, the boy from Poughkeepsie who hadn't made it to Montreal. He thought of his father's grave, and his mother's, and the way he'd never had time to mourn either before the uniforms came calling.

Elisabeth had lit a fire indoors and was baking something sweet, something comforting. He heard the baby crying. One of his girls sang to hush him, out of tune and soft.

Fifty-one, and starting again.

He leaned back and squinted toward the horizon, past the fog, past the river. Past everything he'd lost. There was land waiting west, they said. Land for Loyalists. Land for the broken to become whole again.

He would go. He would bring Elisabeth and the children. He would clear the brush, build up stone, dig the roots deep. Not because he trusted governments, but because the soil had no politics, and the land, at least, kept its promises when a man gave it sweat and time.

The war was over. Now came the harder part—making life from the ashes.

For Authors: Giving Voice to Corporal Herman Samuel Smith

You now hold the threads of a real man who once walked this continent—a man of faith, family, and fierce resilience. Samuel Smith was 51 when the Treaty of Paris was signed, a father of ten, a former Colonel with the Loyal Rangers. He had seen battle and betrayal, and yet he still chose to build.

Ways to Bring Him Into Your Novel:

- **As a patriarchal figure**: Imagine him guiding younger settlers or Loyalist refugees through early Kingston or Sorel, sharing stories of New York, or calming tension in a fledgling Loyalist settlement.

- **As a mentor**: He could advise a younger soldier struggling with grief or the chaos of resettlement.

- **As a husband and father**: His letters and interactions with Elisabeth, worn by the war but determined, would reveal his inner life. His parenting style could show both discipline and tenderness.

- **As a haunted man**: Samuel saw the Revolution fracture families and communities. Let him wrestle with the weight of survival—his guilt, his loyalty, his losses.

Visual Details and Period Tips:

● **Appearance**: At 51, he may have been lean from hardship, face weathered, hair likely powdered or graying naturally, clothes patched from travel. A long military coat, tricorn or round hat, knee breeches, stockings, and worn boots would be accurate. He may have carried a walking stick, not just from age but from injury or terrain.

● **Voice**: Let his speech carry gravitas. He's not a man of florid words but one who chooses them carefully. His faith and years give him dignity; his humour is dry and rooted in common sense.

● **Faith**: Samuel might reference sermons, psalms, or personal faith in his reflections. But don't make him a zealot—his faith was likely private, pragmatic, and worn like a warm cloak.

● **Tools and Items**: A hand-carved pipe, a Bible or prayer book, a worn haversack, military-issued gear repurposed for farming.

Tone Tip: Samuel is not bitter, but neither is he naïve. Write him with humility, wisdom, and the ache of a man who has buried more than he has celebrated—but still stands.

Closing Torch-Passing: I've walked the records, traced his footsteps from Dutchess County to Sorel and back to Poughkeepsie. But you—fellow author—can walk beside him. Lend him your pen, your breath, your fire. Let him speak again. Let readers feel the weight of his boots in the soil of a land not yet a country. Let Samuel Smith live.

www.wikitree.com/wiki/Smith-113880[1]

Elizabeth (Mott) Smith

October 11, 1734 – 1811

Wife of Sergeant Samuel Smith. Loyalist.

Scene: Autumn 1783 – The War Is Over, But Not For Me

The news arrived with the clarity of a church bell ringing on frostbitten air: the Treaty had been signed in Paris. The war was, officially, over.

Elisabeth stood at the window, her hands still coated in flour from kneading the morning's bread, staring at the grey sky above the river. She should have felt something—relief, joy, maybe the lifting of a long-held breath. But she only felt distance. Distance from the homeland she had once known, and from the family she would never be able to see again.

Down the narrow lane, other Loyalists gathered in quiet conversation. The Grass family was preparing to depart for Cataraqui, and Anna Margaretha had stopped by the day before, belly round with her seventh child, her tone hopeful and kind.

"You can still come with us," Anna had offered, her hand resting gently on Elisabeth's arm. "Michael says the land is good. The bay is deep. We'll rebuild, Elisabeth."

But Samuel was too sick to travel. And more than that, she had already missed Amy's wedding.

Amy—her bright, stubborn girl—was to marry Jeremiah Lapp in Queens this month. Elisabeth had embroidered her wedding kerchief years ago, back when Amy was still too young to think of courtship. She had planned to pass it to her on the morning of the wedding. But that day would come and go without her. She would not be there to see Amy walk down the aisle, nor to bless her union. Not as a Loyalist. Not now.

---

1.   http://www.wikitree.com/wiki/Smith-113880

Even her brother Samuel, once so close, had written only once since the war turned sour. He remained in Dutchess County, a soldier under Clinton, firm in his allegiance to the new Republic. He had chosen his path. So had she.

Inside, Anna, her thirteen-year-old, stirred the coals in the hearth. Elisabeth brushed her hands on her apron and turned to the room. She'd borne ten children. Ten. Ten living children, thank God. A miracle in times such as these.

Samuel would later petition for land—350 acres, she had overheard him mumbling in the night. Enough to settle their children if they could ever get to Upper Canada.

She returned to her dough, pressing and folding it with slow, careful rhythm. The war might be over for the politicians and generals, but for women like her, the next battle—of survival, of rebuilding, of loss and faith—had only just begun.

AUTHOR'S SECTION: WRITING Elisabeth (Mott) Smith Into Fiction

Elisabeth's story offers authors a unique lens into the Loyalist experience from the perspective of a strong matriarch left behind. She is not on the frontlines, nor among the first to resettle, but her life is marked by sacrifice, patience, and an unwavering loyalty to family.

Writing Tips:

Elisabeth is a woman of both strength and grief. Show her anchoring a large household while carrying the quiet pain of missed milestones—like her daughter Amy's wedding, which she cannot attend due to her Loyalist status.

Explore her inner life: her faith, her devotion to Samuel, her homesickness for New York, and her loneliness as the only Loyalist among her siblings.

Her friendship with Anna Margaretha Grass offers a narrative bridge between women facing similar challenges. You could even contrast Elisabeth's hesitation with Anna's bold move to Cataraqui.

HISTORICAL CONTEXT & Details:

Her Lutheran upbringing means her faith likely informed much of her worldview. Her days would have been structured by prayer, domestic duties, and church life when possible.

Clothing would have been modest and practical—wool gowns, aprons, fichus (neck scarves), and a cap. As a woman in her late forties, she may also have worn a darker palette or reused older materials.

Despite the trials of war, she had all ten children still living—a rare feat that speaks to her resilience and maternal strength. This fact would have deeply shaped her identity.

THEMES TO EXPLORE:

Displacement and longing: Elisabeth's inability to attend her daughter's wedding offers a powerful symbol of the personal costs of loyalty.

Delayed exodus: Her family does not leave immediately for Canada, giving writers a rich space to explore what life was like for Loyalists still in the American states after the war's end.

Matriarchal wisdom: She is a woman of quiet authority, passing down skills, faith, and resolve to her daughters—and to readers through your pages.

YOU NOW HOLD THE THREADS of Elisabeth's legacy. Her voice may have been quieted in the records, but you, dear author, can stitch it back together—thread by thread, memory by memory.

www.wikitree.com/wiki/Mott-1560[2]

---

2.   http://www.wikitree.com/wiki/Mott-1560

Amy Smith

Character Scene: Amy Smith – Queens, New York, Autumn 1783

The church bell tolled slowly over the rooftops of Queens, drawing a few scattered birds from their perches as Amy adjusted the fall of her shawl. Her fingers trembled—not from nerves about the vows she was about to take, but from the weight of absence.

Her parents were gone. Not gone to death, but gone to exile. Corporal Herman Smith and his wife Elisabeth had fled months earlier, driven out of New York for their steadfast loyalty to the Crown. Amy hadn't heard from them since the spring. Her younger sister Anna had vanished with them. There had been no chance to say goodbye.

Now Amy stood at the threshold of St. George's, the place she had once imagined her mother lacing up her gown, her father standing proud at her side. Instead, her Uncle Maurice—who had served in the 2nd Dutchess County Militia—offered his arm, his expression unreadable beneath the brim of his hat.

He hadn't spoken of Herman. Not once. And though he stood beside Amy now, it was clear the war still smoldered in the silence between them.

Her Aunt Sarah and Aunt Jemima fussed over her hem, over the placement of her veil, doing their best to make the morning feel like joy. But Amy saw the sorrow in their eyes too.

"They would've been here if they could," Aunt Jemima whispered, brushing a curl from Amy's cheek. "Don't you carry even a drop of doubt."

Amy nodded, blinking hard.

Outside, Jeremiah Lapp stood waiting in his best coat, his hat tucked under his arm. The last of the war's banners had only just come down from the streets of Manhattan. Everything was shifting. No one knew what would come next.

But for Amy, today was about planting her feet in this new soil and choosing to grow—even if half her heart was somewhere in the north, imagining her parents whispering a prayer for her across the ocean of exile.

Author's Section: Writing Amy Smith into Fiction

Amy's wedding unfolds in the shadow of loss and separation—not by death, but by forced exile. Her Loyalist parents didn't abandon her; they were driven away, and their absence becomes the emotional core of her story.

Writing Tips:

• Portray Amy as a woman caught between worlds, neither fully Loyalist nor Rebel, trying to carve out a life amidst the fractured remains of her family.

• Her uncle, Maurice, may serve as a foil—he's on the "winning" side but doesn't feel victorious. His silence or distance can deepen the emotional texture.

• Highlight Amy's quiet strength: she honors her parents by holding them in her heart even as she moves forward in their absence.

Setting and Dress Notes: Queens, just after the war, would still carry echoes of both occupation and liberation. The chapel may have been patched up after years of tension.

Amy's wedding attire would reflect simplicity with touches of familial memory: perhaps a ribbon her mother once gave her, or a brooch from her sister. A gown of homespun muslin, with a modest fichu and a kerchief to hold her hair back. The elegance would lie in what is remembered, not displayed.

Supporting Cast for Authors:

- *Maurice Smith*: A man whose patriotism doesn't soothe the ache of a divided family. Writers can use his internal conflict to reflect the nation's own.

- *Sarah Peters & Jemima Sands*: Anchors of female resilience. They are Amy's link to what remains of her family and offer love without pretense.

In Amy's story, you find the quiet heartbreak of a generation torn in half. Her walk down the aisle isn't just a wedding—it's a step toward a life that insists on healing, even when the wounds are still fresh.

Author's Note:

Amy's scene is based on a historically plausible situation: a daughter remaining in New York while her Loyalist family fled to British Canada. While her parents, Herman and Elisabeth Smith, and her younger sister Anna are documented as Loyalists, there are currently no surviving records to confirm whether Amy Smith or her husband, Jeremiah Lapp, were Loyalists themselves. No death records have yet been found for either of them, and although one child's christening record may suggest a Loyalist connection, it remains unconfirmed.

This moment imagines how her Loyalist family might have felt, separated from their daughter on one of the most important days of her life. Scenes like these reflect the deeply personal consequences of civil war—families divided not only by distance but by political allegiance.

Writers are encouraged to explore this family's story from multiple angles and possibilities, acknowledging the uncertainty while honoring the emotional truth experienced by so many families of the time.

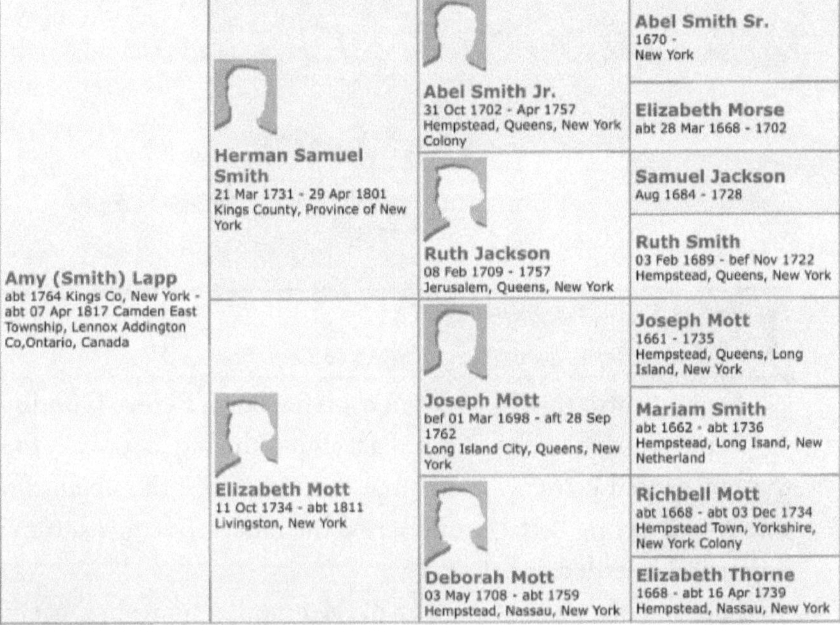

Amy (Smith) Lapp abt 1764 Kings Co, New York - abt 07 Apr 1817 Camden East Township, Lennox Addington Co,Ontario, Canada	**Herman Samuel Smith** 21 Mar 1731 - 29 Apr 1801 Kings County, Province of New York	**Abel Smith Jr.** 31 Oct 1702 - Apr 1757 Hempstead, Queens, New York Colony	**Abel Smith Sr.** 1670 - New York
			Elizabeth Morse abt 28 Mar 1668 - 1702
		Ruth Jackson 08 Feb 1709 - 1757 Jerusalem, Queens, New York	**Samuel Jackson** Aug 1684 - 1728
			Ruth Smith 03 Feb 1689 - bef Nov 1722 Hempstead, Queens, New York
	Elizabeth Mott 11 Oct 1734 - abt 1811 Livingston, New York	**Joseph Mott** bef 01 Mar 1698 - aft 28 Sep 1762 Long Island City, Queens, New York	**Joseph Mott** 1661 - 1735 Hempstead, Queens, Long Island, New York
			Mariam Smith abt 1662 - abt 1736 Hempstead, Long Isand, New Netherland
		Deborah Mott 03 May 1708 - abt 1759 Hempstead, Nassau, New York	**Richbell Mott** abt 1668 - abt 03 Dec 1734 Hempstead Town, Yorkshire, New York Colony
			Elizabeth Thorne 1668 - abt 16 Apr 1739 Hempstead, Nassau, New York

WikiTree.com: The Free Family Tree — Where genealogists collaborate
https://www.wikitree.com/wiki/Smith-127806

Anna Smith

July 5, 1770 – December 25, 1851
Daughter of Loyalists. Witness to Departure.

Scene: Autumn 1783 – The Last Afternoon Before Goodbye

Anna Smith had always loved autumn—the bite in the air, the way the sun slanted golden through the thinning trees, the smell of wood smoke and drying herbs strung across the rafters. But this autumn felt different. Unsettled. Final.

She sat alone on the back step of their modest home in Queens, her hands folded in her lap, a half-done row of embroidery forgotten beside her. Inside, her mother was kneading bread. Her father, still weak from fever, was asleep, his cough rattling like dry corn stalks.

Anna glanced down at the soft fabric in her lap. She had started stitching a kerchief for her sister Amy—something to tuck into her hand as she walked down the aisle, something from home. But there would be no wedding for Anna to attend. No familiar faces. No watching her sister promise herself to Jeremiah Lapp. Amy would walk down the church aisle alone, and Anna would be here, brushing flour off her skirts and pretending she didn't want to cry.

"Thirteen," her mother had said a few nights before, brushing Anna's hair by firelight. "A good age to begin understanding the world."

Anna didn't want to understand the world. She wanted to stay with her sister. With her friends. She wanted her father to get well, her mother to laugh more, and the war to never have happened at all.

But the war was over now. Officially. A treaty signed far away in Paris had decided everything. The rebels had won. And now, Loyalists like her family were leaving. Some had already gone—Mrs. Grass and her children, heading with Captain Grass to a place called Cataraqui, somewhere beyond the edge of the maps Anna had studied in her father's books.

The thought of it thrilled and terrified her in equal measure.

A squirrel darted along the fence, tail flicking, and Anna watched it go. She wondered if the forests in Cataraqui had squirrels. If the trees looked the same. If she'd still dream of Amy's wedding years from now.

She pressed the unfinished kerchief to her face, inhaling the faint scent of lavender. "Goodbye, Amy," she whispered. "I'll remember for both of us."

Author's Section: Writing Anna Smith Into Fiction

Anna Smith, only thirteen at the end of the American Revolution, embodies the youthful perspective of a Loyalist child caught between two worlds. Her age places her at a poignant crossroads—old enough to understand the implications of war and loss, yet young enough to dream of simpler joys.

Writing Tips:

- Anna is a bridge character. Use her as a lens to explore how the Revolution fractured families—not just politically, but emotionally.

- Contrast her admiration for her older sister Amy with the burden of being left behind. Their separation, especially over something as joyful as a wedding, speaks volumes about the quiet sorrow of Loyalist families.

- Consider how her view of Canada evolves over time. As someone who dies in Camden East, Ontario, you can trace her growth from apprehensive girl to matriarch in a new land.

Historical Context & Details:

● At thirteen, Anna may have just begun taking on adult responsibilities—learning to sew, cook, care for younger siblings. The unfinished wedding kerchief is a symbol of her innocence interrupted.

● Life in Camden East would eventually offer stability, but 1783 was filled with uncertainty. As her family waited for Samuel's health to improve, Anna lived in limbo—a rich emotional setting for writers.

● Her clothing would reflect her station: simple dresses in homespun or calico, an apron, perhaps a short gown over a shift, with a kerchief at her neck and a linen cap or bonnet.

Themes to Explore:

● *Coming of age in exile:* Anna's early teens during a mass migration gives her a unique arc, one shaped by displacement, duty, and deferred dreams.

● *Memory and legacy:* She lived until 1851, long enough to witness Canada's formation as a nation-in-the-making. Use that longevity to reflect on the impact of her Loyalist roots.

● *Sisterhood and separation:* Her relationship with Amy—part admiration, part heartbreak—can serve as a deeply humanizing thread in your narrative.

Anna's voice is quiet but enduring. Now, two centuries later, you can carry her memory forward—showing the world that even the smallest hands helped shape the land we now call home. Give her that voice. Tell her story.

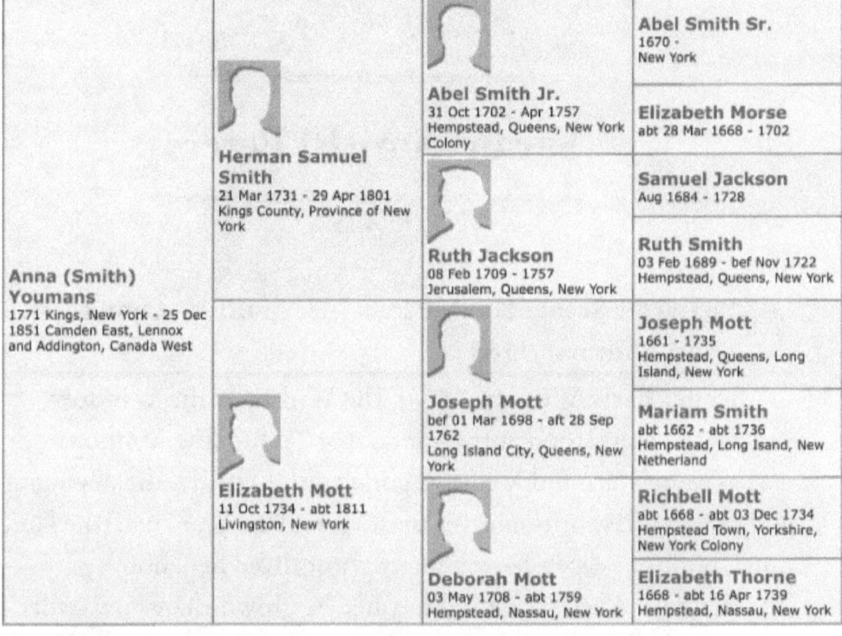
Abel Smith Sr.
1670 -
New York

Abel Smith Jr.
31 Oct 1702 - Apr 1757
Hempstead, Queens, New York Colony

Elizabeth Morse
abt 28 Mar 1668 - 1702

Herman Samuel Smith
21 Mar 1731 - 29 Apr 1801
Kings County, Province of New York

Samuel Jackson
Aug 1684 - 1728

Ruth Jackson
08 Feb 1709 - 1757
Jerusalem, Queens, New York

Ruth Smith
03 Feb 1689 - bef Nov 1722
Hempstead, Queens, New York

Anna (Smith) Youmans
1771 Kings, New York - 25 Dec 1851 Camden East, Lennox and Addington, Canada West

Joseph Mott
1661 - 1735
Hempstead, Queens, Long Island, New York

Joseph Mott
bef 01 Mar 1698 - aft 28 Sep 1762
Long Island City, Queens, New York

Mariam Smith
abt 1662 - abt 1736
Hempstead, Long Isand, New Netherland

Elizabeth Mott
11 Oct 1734 - abt 1811
Livingston, New York

Richbell Mott
abt 1668 - abt 03 Dec 1734
Hempstead Town, Yorkshire, New York Colony

Deborah Mott
03 May 1708 - abt 1759
Hempstead, Nassau, New York

Elizabeth Thorne
1668 - abt 16 Apr 1739
Hempstead, Nassau, New York

Sarah (Smith) Peters

haracter Scene: Sarah Peters (née Smith) – Oyster Bay, New York, Autumn 1783

Scene: Early Winter 1783 – The Widow at the Window

Sarah Peters stood at the window of her modest farmhouse, fingers curled loosely around a teacup gone cold. Outside, the sky hung low and grey, the last brittle leaves twisting on bare branches. The land was quiet, but not peaceful—too many ghosts lived here now.

Her son, Abel, stood behind her. A grown man now, taller than his father had been, with his uncle Maurice's square jaw and his uncle Herman's way of standing at attention even when he wasn't wearing a uniform. He held a letter in his hand—creased, smudged from travel.

"It's over," he said gently. "They signed it. The war's finished."

Sarah didn't answer right away. She just kept her eyes on the horizon, where the woods faded into the cold mist. A war couldn't be finished, not really. Not when the table was still missing chairs. Not when brothers on opposite sides of the battlefield had once shared a cradle.

"Over," she whispered. "Then let it be over. Let the dead rest, and the living stop choosing sides."

She turned from the window and reached for Abel's hand, the same hand that had once clutched hers to cross a stream, now roughened by work and war and adulthood.

"Your Uncle Maurice will still wear his colors. Your Uncle Herman will never set foot on this land again." Her voice cracked but did not break. "But maybe your children won't have to ask why."

Abel looked at her, unsure how to respond. She smiled then, faintly, her eyes shining but dry.

"Go fetch the others. We'll have a proper meal tonight. If the war is done, let's make something of the peace."

She set the cup down and began clearing the table—an act so ordinary, so rooted in survival, it felt like prayer.

Outside, the wind carried the faint sound of birdsong, as if the land itself were trying to remember how to sing again.

Author's Section: Writing Sarah Peters Into Fiction

Overview:

Sarah Peters is the quiet strength beneath the storm—widowed before the war was even over, caught between two beloved brothers on opposite sides. Born into a divided family and married to a man who avoided official allegiances, Sarah represents the many women whose lives were shattered not by battlefield muskets, but by absence, tension, and endurance.

Writing Tips:

Sarah is not dramatic. She's steady, tired, dignified. Her pain runs deep, but she carries it with grace. Let her emotions rise subtly: the way she touches her husband's chair, how she listens before she speaks, how her eyes say more than her words.

Use her as a bridge character—between generations, between divided families, between war and peace.

Her wisdom should feel earned. She isn't bitter, but she has seen enough not to be naïve.

CHARACTER POSSIBILITIES:

She could be a matriarch trying to hold a fractured family together, keeping traditions alive while everything around her changes.

Perhaps she tends a hidden grave—her husband George's—or keeps a secret letter from one of her brothers.

Her son Abel could become a character of moral struggle, shaped by his mother's quiet resilience and haunted by the legacy of the war that defined his uncles.

HISTORICAL CLOTHING & Details:

She would wear a simple homespun gown, perhaps darkened in tone out of mourning. An apron stained from years of use. Her hair tied back in a practical cap.

Her hands would be worn—knitting, mending, chopping wood if needed.

Her farmhouse might have Loyalist keepsakes tucked in corners... and maybe a rebel's letter hidden in a box beneath the floorboards.

THEMES TO EXPLORE:

Endurance and grief: Her husband died before peace came, and she lived through the war's final years in loneliness and fear. But she endures, and in that endurance is hope.

Family divided by war: Her brothers symbolize the brutal cost of ideology in a civil conflict. She does not take sides, but she bears the scars of both.

A woman's place in memory: Sarah didn't wear a uniform. But without women like her, the home would have fallen. Her life is a testament to survival.

LET SARAH PETERS STAND in your story as the voice of all the women who waited, wept, and worked while men wrote history with swords. Let her remind readers that peace isn't a treaty—it's the act of setting a table again, of welcoming home a son, of choosing to live. Even when the world forgets her, you don't have to.

Sarah (Smith) Peters	Abel Smith Jr.	Abel Smith Sr.	John Smith
31 Oct 1732 Oyster Bay, Nassau, Province of New York - 27 Mar 1780 Pleasant Valley, Dutchess, Province of New York	**Abel Smith Jr.** 31 Oct 1702 - Apr 1757 Hempstead, Queens, New York Colony	**Abel Smith Sr.** 1670 - New York	**John Smith** abt 1624 - 1719 England
			Sara Strickland aft 1620 - New York
		Elizabeth Morse abt 28 Mar 1668 - 1702	[Great-Grandfather?]
			[Great-Grandmother?]
	Ruth Jackson 08 Feb 1709 - 1757 Jerusalem, Queens, New York	**Samuel Jackson** Aug 1684 - 1728	**John Jackson** abt 1645 - bef 06 Dec 1725 Hempstead, Queens, Long Island, New York
			Elizabeth Seaman abt 1653 - 26 Aug 1724 Hempstead, Queens, Long Island, New York Colony
		Ruth Smith 03 Feb 1689 - bef Nov 1722 Hempstead, Queens, New York	[Great-Grandfather?]
			[Great-Grandmother?]

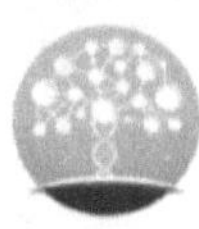

WikiTree.com: The Free Family Tree — Where genealogists collaborate
https://www.wikitree.com/wiki/Smith-110379

Abel Peters

Scene: Late 1783 – A Man Between Two Worlds

The soil clung stubbornly to Abel Peters' boots as he crossed the edge of the field. Frost had kissed the last of the cornstalks, and the air had that hollow stillness that came after the final harvest. The peace had come—not with joy, not with jubilation, but with silence. He carried the silence like a stone in his chest.

His wife, Sarah, was shelling peas by the fire. Inside, the children played quietly, sensing something had changed though they didn't yet know the shape of it.

Abel paused by the woodpile, splitting logs in steady rhythm. Chop. Turn. Split. He worked like a man who had been waiting years for permission to breathe—and didn't quite trust it.

"Uncle Herman won't be coming back," he said aloud, though no one was there to hear. "Not even to say goodbye."

It had been a letter, smuggled up through friends of friends. Herman was with the Loyalists, far north, safe perhaps, but exiled forever from this land—this soil their family had worked for generations. And little Anna—twelve and bright-eyed—was gone with him. Abel had watched her grow like a sapling between storms. She had clutched his hand at church just two summers past. Now she'd become a shadow in another province, on another side of the war.

He thought, too, of Uncle Maurice—still here, still fighting in words even after muskets had gone silent. Maurice had chosen the rebel cause, and though the fighting was done, his bitterness hadn't ended.

Abel rubbed the back of his neck, staring toward the tree line. He had buried his father in 1780 without knowing if the war would ever end. Now, with peace signed, there was no family feast, no homecoming. Just absences.

"I didn't fight," he muttered. "But I lost all the same."

He picked up a fresh log and split it clean down the middle.

"But I'll plant the orchard next spring. For my children. For hers."

He didn't know if Anna Smith would remember him. Maybe one day she'd return. Maybe not. But the land was still here. The fields still needed tending.

He would hold the line, as his mother had. He would not let the roots die.

AUTHOR'S SECTION: WRITING Abel Peters Into Fiction

Abel Peters represents the silent, unlisted majority—the ones who stayed, who neither fled nor fought, whose war was fought in whispers and glances, in empty seats at the table and names never spoken aloud again. He is the son of George and Sarah Peters (née Smith), born into a family split by war. His mother's brother Herman joined the Loyalists and can never return. Another uncle, Maurice, fought with the Patriot militia. Abel chose neither side—or perhaps, like so many, he had no choice at all.

Writing Tips:

Abel is a character of quiet moral weight. He didn't march with a flag, but every decision he made was political in its own right—who he spoke to, who he traded with, whose names he dared mention aloud.

He is not neutral, he is torn. Abel carries the weight of a mother's grief for a banished brother, and the unspoken guilt of surviving without choosing a side.

Use him to show how conflict lingers in the lives of those who stayed behind. His world is quieter after the war—but it is also lonelier.

His death in New York marks him as rooted, a man who kept to his land and his people, even as those people drifted or disappeared.

HISTORICAL DETAILS & Family Connections:

Born in colonial Hempstead or nearby, Abel likely worked the family farm and continued doing so through the years of conflict.

With no records of military service, Abel is among the invisible many—common men who endured, labored, and buried their losses without headlines.

His cousin Anna Smith (age 12 in 1783) was likely someone he remembered fondly—perhaps a girl who helped in the kitchen, who disappeared one day when her family followed Herman north.

If his wife, also named Sarah, lost family to the Loyalist cause, this bond would have deepened their shared grief.

He may have lived with a quiet hope that one day, they would all return.

THEMES TO EXPLORE:

Loyalty to family over politics: Abel is torn between his mother's Loyalist brother and his Patriot uncle—men he once saw as equals, now turned enemies by circumstance.

Home as a battlefield: His war was not on the front lines, but in the silence that filled the farm once letters stopped coming.

Bitterness vs. peace: He may resent the war for what it took, but he also may feel relief that he stayed behind. He didn't choose a side, but he didn't lose everything, either.

Hope and quiet resistance: Abel might pass stories to his children—stories that keep both uncles alive in memory, refusing to let war erase either one.

SYMBOLIC MOTIFS:

A ledger with names struck through: Friends who left for New Brunswick, family who disappeared—Abel keeps the books, even if he never speaks the names aloud.

The orchard never quite harvested: Symbol of work left undone, of potential that went north, or never came back from the field.

The empty barn loft: Once filled with cousins at harvest time. Now silent.

LEGACY: ABEL PETERS belongs to the middle—a man who lived through the war, but not by fighting it. He held the land while others claimed titles. His hands bore the marks of survival, not victory. And in the end, when the world began again, it was men like Abel who taught the children how to plant again, how to stay, and how to remember without bitterness.

			William Valentine Peters abt 1650 -
		Charles Peters M.D. abt 1678 - 03 Apr 1733 Cornwall, England	Ann Unknown abt 1658 - St. Clement, Dane,London
	George Peters 13 Apr 1726 - 27 Mar 1780 Hempstead, Nassau County, Province of New York		George Hewlett Sr. abt 1634 - 14 May 1722 England
		Mary Hewlett 1689 - 1744 Long Island, New York,	Mary Bayless 1645 - 1733 Jamaica, Long Island, New Netherland
Abel Peters - 29 Nov 1799 Clinton, Dutchess, New York, United States			Abel Smith Sr. 1670 - New York
	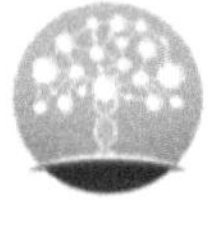 Sarah Smith 31 Oct 1732 - 27 Mar 1780 Oyster Bay, Nassau, Province of New York	Abel Smith Jr. 31 Oct 1702 - Apr 1757 Hempstead, Queens, New York Colony	Elizabeth Morse abt 28 Mar 1668 - 1702
			Samuel Jackson Aug 1684 - 1728
		Ruth Jackson 08 Feb 1709 - 1757 Jerusalem, Queens, New York	Ruth Smith 03 Feb 1689 - bef Nov 1722 Hempstead, Queens, New Yo

Maurice Smith

Character Scene: Maurice Smith – Hempstead, New York, Autumn 1783

The news came on the heels of frost—quiet, brittle, and final. The war was over.

Maurice Smith stood in the field behind his modest home, calloused hands resting on the haft of his hoe, though the soil was hard and the harvest already in. Mary had come running from the village green, her cloak flapping like a banner behind her, cheeks red from the wind and the words she couldn't wait to speak.

"They've signed it, Maurice," she'd said breathlessly, clutching his arm. "It's done. The war is over."

He hadn't answered right away. Just stared past her toward the far woodline, where the trees stood dark and quiet and the world seemed to exhale.

"Over," he repeated now, more to himself. "After all this time."

He was forty-seven. A private in the Dutchess County Militia. A man who had held the line in the cold, prayed beside bloodied comrades, and watched friends disappear into shadow—some to death, some to the north, like his brother Herman.

Herman had chosen the Crown. Maurice had stayed.

They'd never spoken again.

He leaned against the hoe, the handle pressing into his ribs like the memory of a musket's weight. He didn't feel triumphant. Not really. Just... tired. The sort of tired that came from too many years with teeth clenched and eyes always watching for smoke.

Behind him, Mary called his name softly, holding out a shawl against the evening chill.

He took it, folding it over his shoulders like a soldier's blanket. Then, wordless, he turned and walked toward her, toward home. Toward whatever peace might come next.

Author's Section: Writing Maurice Smith into Fiction

Maurice Smith is the kind of Revolutionary War character who deserves more attention: not a general, not a traitor, not a legend—just a man. A farmer, a militiaman, a brother divided from a brother by politics and principle.

Writing Tips:

- Maurice is grounded in place. He chose to stay in New York, perhaps out of loyalty to his neighbors or a desire to avoid upheaval. He might not have loved the Continental Congress, but he believed in defending his home.

- Use his internal conflict to explore themes of divided families. He still wonders what became of Herman. He still wonders if he chose right.

- He is deeply human, a man of quiet courage. His scenes are best written with restraint—subtle emotions, earthy language, deeply felt loyalties.

Clothing and Appearance:

As a working farmer and former militiaman, Maurice likely wore coarse breeches, wool stockings, a linen shirt, and a waistcoat patched from years of wear. His hands would be sun-darkened and strong. In colder months, he'd don a greatcoat or cape. He wore the garments of a man who worked the land—practical, sturdy, and unadorned.

Maurice is a rich addition to any Revolutionary War narrative: a man with dirt under his nails and ghosts in his eyes. Through him, writers can explore the moral gray zones of revolution, the weight of duty, and the fragile hope that, when war ends, something better might still be built.

www.wikitree.com/wiki/Smith-29650[1]

---

1.   http://www.wikitree.com/wiki/Smith-29650

Jemima (Smith) Sands

Character Scene: Jemima Smith Sands – New York Colony, Autumn 1783

The war was over, they said.

Jemima Sands stood still by the open window, the chill of late autumn sliding in beneath her sleeves. The leaves outside tumbled like memories—gold, brown, and gone. Her husband George was in the yard splitting wood, the steady thud of the axe a rhythm she'd come to depend on these last long years.

She didn't weep. Nor did she cheer. She only listened.

"Over," she murmured, as if saying it aloud would make it real. "It's over."

She was forty-four, not yet old, but aged in the way war ages those who wait. She'd buried neighbors. She'd seen boys leave home and come back men—or not come back at all. She'd written to her brothers and received nothing but silence in return. Maurice had joined the Patriot militia. Herman, her youngest brother, had stayed loyal to the Crown and disappeared north with the other Loyalists. She hadn't heard from him in years. She didn't know if he was alive.

The end of war did not bring answers. Only quiet. Only questions.

Behind her, the hearth glowed. Supper simmered. Her children would be in soon, asking what came next. Jemima had no answer for that either. Her world had been stitched together by faith, family, and the rhythm of seasons. War had torn at that fabric, but she'd held it together—barely.

"George," she called softly, and he turned, nodding. "Supper."

There would be peace, perhaps. But she had learned to be cautious with hope.

Author's Section: Writing Jemima Smith Sands into Fiction

Jemima is the kind of woman history often forgets: quietly heroic, living between lines drawn by men at war. As the sister of both a Loyalist (Corporal Herman Samuel Smith) and a Patriot (Private Maurice Smith), her experience embodies the emotional fracture of revolution.

Writing Tips:

- Explore how divided families navigated the emotional strain of war. Jemima may have felt like a bridge no one wanted to cross.

- She is not overtly political, but she is deeply loyal—to her family, her home, and to peace.

- Use her as a touchstone for domestic war stories: the waiting, the worry, the resilience.

Clothing and Appearance: As a 44-year-old woman living in rural New York during the late 18th century, Jemima's clothing would reflect practicality with modest style. A fitted bodice over a linen shift, full skirts of muted color, and an apron would be daily wear. A simple cotton or muslin cap would keep her hair tidy. If she owned finer garments, they would likely be stored away for Sunday or visits.

Writing Jemima gives voice to the many women who kept homes, raised children, and waited for letters that never came. She reminds readers that not all wars are fought with muskets—some are fought with memory, silence, and strength.

www.wikitree.com/wiki/Smith-327752[1]

---

1.   http://www.wikitree.com/wiki/Smith-327752

Command Beneath the Canvas: The Loyalist Commodores

Introduction:

They were not soldiers in red, nor did they march with musket and drum—but the Commodores bore the weight of the Crown just the same. On water, not land, they carved out the Loyalist legacy, steering battered bateaux and makeshift flotillas through rivers thick with ice and fog. These were men who commanded not fleets of warships, but lifelines—ferrying the displaced, the wounded, the stubbornly loyal, and every earthly possession they dared salvage from a country that had turned against them.

The war may have ended in 1783, but their hardest journeys came after. When the British withdrew, it was the Commodores who stayed behind long enough to carry out the retreat. They shepherded families through uncertain currents, navigating not just rapids and lakes, but grief, fear, and the dizzying weight of beginning again.

In Kingston and across the water routes of Upper Canada, their names were recorded not in victory rolls, but in shipping logs, paylists, and petitions. And yet, without them, there would have been no Loyalist settlement—only scattered refugees and broken promises.

This chapter honours the Commodores: the quiet captains of exile and survival.

Commodore David Betton

D. *October 11, 1794 – Kingston, Upper Canada*
Master of the Waters. Loyal to the End.

Scene: Fall 1783 – The Stillness After the Storm

The wind was calm that morning, but David Betton still stood as though bracing against a storm. One hand rested lightly on the rail of the docked schooner, the other gripped the rolled parchment that had arrived just hours before. He had read it once. Then again. And once more, though it didn't change with each pass. The war was over.

He could taste it—like iron in the air, like gunpowder residue in the back of the throat. The Treaty of Paris had been signed. The fight, after all these years, was officially finished. The King had ceded ground. The rebels had their victory. And what was left for men like him?

He stared out over the water, the familiar blue-grey expanse of Lake Ontario mirroring the skies above. It was not the Atlantic. It was not home. But it would have to do.

"Commodore?" a younger voice called from the pier behind him.

Betton didn't turn. "They've signed it," he said, voice low, worn like the edge of an old blade. "It's done."

The boy—barely out of youth—stood a little straighter. "What happens now, sir?"

Betton inhaled deeply, the wind shifting just enough to lift the edge of his greatcoat. "Now? We build. We begin again, in loyalty, and in memory of what was lost."

He was no longer a young officer chasing tides and titles. His days of command under the Union Jack had changed with the continent.

But he still had his men, his name, and his cause. If this was exile, so be it. He would make of it a haven.

His eyes scanned the horizon. He thought of the ships burned in retreat, the loyal families who'd packed what little they could carry, and the names of comrades whose graves were now behind enemy lines. He'd never forget them. And Kingston—this little, wind-bitten outpost—would become something they could all be proud of.

"It's the end of a war," Betton said aloud, not to the boy, but to the lake. "But not the end of us."

Author's Section: Writing Commodore David Betton Into Fiction

Commodore Betton represents the stalwart backbone of Loyalist leadership—experienced, deliberate, and forged by conflict. His naval rank gives him gravitas, while his later years in Kingston hint at the quiet legacy of those who helped build postwar Canada from the ground up.

Writing Tips:

● Position Betton as a mentor figure—he's the kind of man younger Loyalists would look to for wisdom, strategy, and steadiness. Use him to deliver truths others are too afraid to voice.

● Explore his emotional layers. He's not simply "stoic." Beneath his ironclad loyalty lies sorrow, anger, and a deep sense of responsibility to those who followed him north.

● Consider how the vastness of water mirrors his interior life: solitude, control, and change. His relationship with ships, weather, and command could be central themes in his portrayal.

Historical Clothing & Details:

- As a Commodore and gentleman, he would likely have worn a well-tailored naval coat—dark blue with brass buttons—over breeches and a waistcoat. He may have retained his tricorn hat and cravat out of tradition and dignity.

- Betton would be skilled in ship handling, cartography, and Loyalist military structure. He likely had dealings with both the Royal Navy and the Provincial Marine.

- By 1783, he would've already been a senior man. Consider his growing awareness of mortality and legacy—especially as he witnessed a new colony forming before his eyes.

Themes to Explore:

- *Legacy and exile:* Betton didn't just lose a war—he lost a homeland. Writers can explore how a man reshapes identity in the ashes of defeat.

- *Loyalist community-building:* He didn't retreat into obscurity. His death in Kingston in 1794 places him as one of the early civic and naval contributors to Upper Canada.

- *Father-figure archetype:* Whether or not you write him with children of his own, Betton is a figure who commands respect. He represents the steadying presence in times of chaos.

David Betton stood at the helm of loyalty when the tide turned—and now, centuries later, you hold the chart in your hands. Give him a voice. Let the lake remember.
www.wikitree.com/wiki/Betton-58[1]

---

1. http://www.wikitree.com/wiki/Betton-58

Captains of Two Wars: One Fought with Arms, the Other with Endurance

Introduction:

The captains who followed the Loyalist cause found themselves at the crossroads of two very different wars. The first was waged with muskets and loyalty to the Crown—a war of smoke, loss, and impossible choices. The second came after the Treaty of Paris inked peace on foreign soil, while here, on the edges of Upper Canada, another campaign began: survival, settlement, and starting again.

These men had led companies through rebellion and retreat. They had answered to their superior officers, faced down fire, and held lines that others abandoned. When the regiments disbanded, they did not disappear. Many took their commissions with them into the wilderness, still guiding, still guarding—this time over families and strangers who looked to them for strength.

Their rank afforded them respect, but it also placed a heavy burden on their shoulders. They were often the first to act, to organize, to petition for land not for themselves alone but for the families that depended on them. They weren't just given land; they earned it daily in sweat, sorrow, and stubborn resolve.

In this chapter, we walk beside the captains—past and present—as they emerge from one kind of war into another. Their names mark the transition from Loyalist soldiers to Canadian founders. Their stories remind us that a true captain never stops leading, no matter the terrain.

Lieutenants in the Wilderness: Duty Beyond the Battlefield

Introduction:

The war may have ended with treaties and signatures in Paris, but for the Lieutenants of the Loyalist regiments, the road ahead remained marked by conflict—only now, it was against hunger, weather, and uncertainty.

They had once been junior officers, responsible for discipline, order, and morale in the ranks. Many were young, ambitious, and caught between loyalty to king and kin. They led skirmishes, carried orders down the chain of command, and watched friends fall in lands they once called home. By the time they reached the northern frontier, they were no longer simply officers—they were survivors.

Here in Upper Canada, the wilderness became their new battleground. The title of Lieutenant still carried weight, but now it meant organizing settlers, marking out roads, and reporting to magistrates instead of generals. These men often acted as the bridge between seasoned captains and the raw, weary Loyalist families just off the boats. They knew the burden of authority, but also the exhaustion of obedience.

They were the quiet architects of order in the chaos that followed war. Whether they stayed in uniform or laid down their swords for axes and ledgers, their role remained vital. They lent structure to a scattered people. Their loyalty did not end with surrender—it transformed into stewardship.

This chapter remembers the Lieutenants: not just for the battles they fought, but for the way they stayed—steadfast in duty, long after the drums of war had fallen silent.

Hugh Earl

*B*orn 1765, Rome, New York Colony – Died January 28, 1841, Kingston, Upper Canada

Young Loyalist, Future Husband of Anne Johnson and Commander in the War of 1812.

Scene: Autumn, 1783 – Loyalist Encampment Outside Montreal

The announcement came just after sunrise. A courier on horseback shouted it down the line as if it were a rumor: "The war's over! Treaty's signed in Paris!"

Hugh Earl stood still, barely breathing, as the meaning sank in. He was eighteen, and the war had filled every corner of his world since he was a boy. It had uprooted his family from Rome, carved neighbors into enemies, burned their fields to ash.

And now? Now there was peace?

He looked toward the edge of the camp where Captain Grass was speaking to a small gathering. Men and women were already forming up to follow him into the wild unknown—Cataraqui, they called it. The ruins of old Fort Frontenac, and the land beyond. There was nothing there but trees, water, and the dream of a second beginning.

He clenched his jaw. "This isn't peace," he said under his breath. "This is exile."

But even as he said it, he knew he'd go. What choice was there? Home was gone. What remained was to build something better.

Later, in the quiet of the evening, he sat beside the fire and thought of her—Anne. The girl with fierce eyes and quiet strength. The daughter of Sir William Johnson and Molly Brant, whose blood carried two worlds, two nations, two histories. They had known each other in Rome. Her voice had calmed him when the world turned to chaos.

He held onto the dream that together, they'd raise children who belonged to no empire but the one they built themselves.

The war was over. But Hugh Earl's real fight was just beginning.

Author's Section: Writing Commander Hugh Earl Into Fiction

Hugh Earl offers an extraordinary opportunity for historical fiction rooted in both youth and resilience. He represents the Loyalist generation who came of age in chaos and found their manhood in the founding of a new land.

His Marriage to Anne Johnson (1791):

This union is both symbolic and rich in historical meaning. Anne, daughter of Sir William Henry Johnson, 1st Baronet and Molly Brant, bridges British and Mohawk heritage. Their marriage in Rome, New York Colony, reflects a blend of loyalties, cultures, and identities rarely explored in depth in Loyalist fiction.

How to Use Him in Fiction:

- As a Loyalist youth navigating the aftermath of revolution and falling in love with a woman from two worlds.

- As a voice of reason and quiet strength in a frontier community still defining itself.

- In later life, as a commander and elder—perhaps helping guide new settlers, or defending the land he once fled to.

What He May Have Worn:

- A well-patched militia coat over simple linen, leather braces and boots hardened by the march.

- Possibly a tricorn hat or wool cap; a powder horn slung across his shoulder.

- A handmade token from Anne—perhaps a braid of sweetgrass or a string of beads she gave him before their parting.

Themes to Explore:

- *The cost of loyalty:* What it means to stay true when it means losing everything.

- *Cross-cultural marriage:* The complexities and strengths of marrying into the Mohawk-British lineage of Anne Johnson.

- *Land and legacy:* Building a new life from nothing, with memory and loss never far behind.

Torch for Authors: Hugh and Anne's love story could form the heart of a sweeping Loyalist epic—a tale of war-torn youth, cultural crossroads, and perseverance in the face of exile. Through them, readers can explore both the colonial and Indigenous experiences of displacement and rebirth in early Upper Canada.
www.wikitree.com/wiki/Earl-1631[1]

---

1. http://www.wikitree.com/wiki/Earl-1631

Lieutenant William MacKay

D*ied March 1801, Kingston, Upper Canada*
Veteran Loyalist Officer, Settler of Cataraqui

Scene: Autumn, 1783 – Loyalist Barracks, Sorel

He read the dispatch twice, lips moving without sound. The Treaty of Paris. Signed. Ratified. Final.

The war was over.

Lieutenant William MacKay folded the parchment with rigid precision and set it on the table before him. His hand rested there a moment, steady but pale. In the firelight, the burnished edge of his officer's sword caught the glow—unused now, but not unhonoured.

He'd given everything to the Crown. Friends, property, the long security of home. He had fought with dignity, yes, but also with grief—grief that he carried now like an old injury that would never heal.

Outside, younger men were shouting. Joy, disbelief, anger—it was all muddled together. William did not join them. Instead, he stood and stepped to the narrow window, looking toward the St. Lawrence, where longboats bobbed in the current, waiting for orders.

Peace, they called it. But peace didn't look like what he'd imagined. It looked like cold water and ruined uniforms, empty pockets and winter soil too hard to till. They were promised land, yes—but the land was forest, rock, and memory.

Still, he had made his decision long ago: he would follow Captain Grass to Cataraqui. He would help build a town from the stones of

Fort Frontenac's ghost. He would die with honour in the service of something enduring—even if no monument ever bore his name.

And he would do it quietly.

He touched the edge of his commission with reverence and turned back toward his gear. The war was over. His duty was not.

Author's Section: Writing Lieutenant William MacKay Into Fiction

Who He Was:

William MacKay was one of many middle-ranking Loyalist officers—educated, dutiful, often older than the settlers he helped guide into exile. A figure of calm discipline, he'd be a stabilizing presence in any narrative about the Loyalist exodus to Cataraqui.

Where He Belongs in Fiction:

- As an officer loyal to Captain Michael Grass, perhaps second-in-command or a quartermaster with intimate knowledge of logistics and terrain.

- As a widower or quiet family man who becomes a father figure to younger settlers, including war orphans or refugees.

- As a keeper of memory—perhaps he writes letters home, keeps a journal, or acts as a source of Loyalist oral history.

What He May Have Worn:

- A faded red officer's coat patched at the elbows, brass buttons dulled by time.

- Sturdy breeches and leather boots worn from campaign life.

- A small notebook or map pouch always at his side, and a ring or locket that ties him to a family he lost or left behind.

Themes to Explore:

- *Dignity in exile:* How does a man used to command retain honour after surrender?

- *Building legacy:* How does a soldier build peace with his hands after years of war?

- *Quiet leadership:* How do the unsung officers keep hope alive for younger settlers?

Torch for Authors: Lieutenant MacKay can serve as a stoic, melancholic mentor in your Loyalist fiction. He's the kind of character readers will trust instinctively—the kind whose death years later in Kingston will feel like the loss of a generation. He might not speak often, but when he does, his words could carry the weight of a dying world—and the seeds of a new one.

www.wikitree.com/wiki/MacKay-5436[1]

---

1.   http://www.wikitree.com/wiki/MacKay-5436

Samuel "Sam" Hewett

Born c. 1740s – Died before March 1809, likely in Kingston, Upper Canada

Settler, Loyalist Veteran, Husband to a Strong Woman Who Survived Him

SCENE: AUTUMN 1783 – Encampment Along the St. Lawrence

The war was done. Not won. Just... done.

Sam Hewett sat on a rough stump near the campfire, a battered tin cup cradled in his hands. His face, weathered from decades of hard work and harder choices, bore a kind of quiet resignation. He wasn't a man of many words—he left speeches to officers and parsons—but the news that the Treaty had been signed brought a deep silence to his bones.

He glanced toward his wife, busy at the fire with other women, boiling beans in a cracked iron pot. The baby on her hip wasn't theirs—they'd never had children of their own—but she held the little one as if it were a promise. That tenderness. That strength. It made Sam feel both grateful and guilty.

"We'll follow Grass," he murmured, mostly to himself.

No one had asked him. He wasn't an officer or leader. Just a farmer with more scars than acres. But Cataraqui—that wild place he'd once heard of during the old campaigns—was as good a place as any to begin again.

He'd carve land for her. Lay foundation stones. Raise a roof if it killed him.

He never wanted her to want for anything. But even then, deep in his chest, he feared he wouldn't live long enough to see it through.

AUTHOR'S SECTION: WRITING Sam Hewett Into Fiction

Who He Was:

Sam Hewett may be almost invisible in the historical record, but that's exactly why he matters. He represents the thousands of Loyalist settlers whose names were never engraved in stone, but whose sweat, sacrifice, and quiet love built the bones of Upper Canada. His story lives on through one powerful entry: his wife, seeking land after his death, still standing her ground in 1809.

Where He Belongs in Fiction:

As a loyal follower of Captain Grass, perhaps a former militiaman or a humble settler who once served under arms in a forgotten regiment.

As a devoted husband, perhaps older than his wife, with a kind but reserved manner.

As a man worn thin by loss, proud but without vanity, ready to give everything to ensure his wife has a future.

WHAT HE MAY HAVE WORN:

A plain linen shirt, sleeves rolled, collar frayed with wear.

Homespun wool trousers, patched at the knee.

A leather vest with pockets for tools, seeds, or a keepsake from home—perhaps a carved charm or folded paper prayer.

No uniform—he was a man of the soil, not the sword.

THEMES TO EXPLORE:

Unrecorded sacrifice: Sam is the kind of character who dies between the lines of history, but his absence shapes the land just as much as the famous names.

Quiet resilience: His strength isn't in battle but in persistence—showing up, enduring, planting hope.

Love in exile: A tender, gritty love story could be drawn from the bond between him and his wife, a woman who later dares to claim land beside Captain Grass himself.

TORCH FOR AUTHORS: Sam Hewett might never speak more than a paragraph in a novel—but oh, how readers will feel him. He's the soul of a new world being born out of the ashes of war. And when you write his widow in 1809, standing alone and petitioning for Lot No. 2, imagine the ghost of Sam beside her. Not gone. Just waiting for her to come home.

www.wikitree.com/wiki/Hewett-2157[1]

---

1.   http://www.wikitree.com/wiki/Hewett-2157

Mrs. Sam Hewett

B orn c. 1740s–1750s – Died after March 1809, likely in Kingston Township, Upper Canada
Loyalist Widow, Land Petitioner, Quiet Pioneer

SCENE: NEW YORK – LATE 1783

News of the peace treaty reaches the Loyalist quarters.

It was over. That's what they were saying.

Men shouted in the streets, some in celebration, others in fury. The British had signed it. The ink was still drying, they claimed. The war was done. The colonies were free. And she—she was a stranger in her own country now.

Mrs. Sam Hewett didn't cheer. She didn't cry. She went to the hearth, stirred the pot as if nothing had changed. But inside, her body tensed as if something had broken loose. Peace—they called it that. But it wasn't peace for her. Not when it meant her neighbors could seize her property. Not when it meant the cause her husband had bled for was dismissed as a mistake. Not when it meant they'd have to leave.

She turned her head slightly when her husband entered. He wasn't well—hadn't been since the fever in late summer. His eyes met hers, the same unspoken thought passing between them.

We won't die here. We won't be buried in this soil.

They had no children to pass the land to. No one to keep the house. No future here. The only thing they had was loyalty—now branded as treason.

She reached for the Bible, its corners soft from use, and whispered the only prayer that came to her:

Let me not be forgotten, Lord. Let the land remember me.

AUTHOR'S SECTION: WRITING Mrs. Sam Hewett Into Fiction

Her War's End:

The end of the war wasn't a joyful relief—it was exile. She wouldn't celebrate with the victors. She would pack quietly, grieve the soil that had once fed her, and turn her back on the only home she had ever known. A Loyalist, with no name on the public record—just "Mrs. Sam Hewett." But she made her own history in that moment by surviving it.

Her Role in Storytelling:

She is the last to pack, not because she's sentimental, but because she knows there's no going back.

She may be among the first to arrive in Kingston, or one of the women left waiting until her husband is well enough to travel. Either way, her choice is bold: she chooses loyalty over safety, silence over betrayal.

She may befriend other Loyalist wives—Anna Grass, Elisabeth Mott—quiet conversations over boiling kettles and drying boots, sharing griefs that history won't record.

WHAT SHE MAY HAVE CARRIED:

A linen pouch with soil from her garden.

Her marriage license, tucked inside her Bible.

A letter from her husband to a now-vanished Loyalist regiment.

A single pair of shoes, resoled twice.

TORCH FOR AUTHORS:

Here is a woman whose name history failed to record—but whose presence shaped a nation. She walked away from everything familiar not in protest, but in faith. She may have lost a homeland, but she claimed a legacy.

Write her as she was: a ghost in the margins, and a flame that refuses to be put out.

www.wikitree.com/wiki/Unknown-718528[1]

---

1.   http://www.wikitree.com/wiki/Unknown-718528

S. Allan McLean

B *orn: [Date unknown], likely in British Colonial America
Died: After February 1804, Upper Canada*

Scene: News of the Official End of the War, 1783

The parchment trembled slightly in his hands, though the winter wind had not yet stirred. Word had come—official, unarguable—that the war was over. The ink still drying on treaties across the sea could never fully capture the weight of it. For S. Allan McLean, standing outside the makeshift quarters in what had once been wilderness and now hinted at becoming Kingston, it was a silence more deafening than cannon fire.

He looked up toward the north, eyes narrowing at the promise of snow. Peace, they called it. Yet the ache in his chest reminded him it was not so simple. Peace meant judgment. Peace meant sorting through who had lost more—loyalty or liberty.

He'd stayed true, and now here he was among others who had paid that same price. Some had titles. Some had only names. But all of them had left behind fields, brothers, childhood homes, and buried kin.

He folded the letter slowly and nodded to the horizon, as if saluting the ghosts of both past and future. "We start again," he said, the words swallowed by the wind.

Author's Section: Writing S. Allan McLean into Fiction

S. Allan McLean is a character with the potential for quiet depth and resilience. While records of his birth and death remain scarce, we know he was present in Kingston Township by 1804 and involved in land dealings alongside prominent Loyalist figures like Captain Grass.

His story invites exploration of what it meant to carry one's identity across battle lines and borders.

Writing Tips:

- Let him serve as a bridge between the old world and the new, with land as both literal and symbolic inheritance.

- Reflect on the emotional complexity of peace: relief, bitterness, hope, and haunting.

- He may be imagined as practical, introspective, loyal to his cause but thoughtful about its cost.

- Give him a voice shaped by disillusionment but driven by duty.

Historical Details to Consider:

- As a Loyalist surveyor, McLean may have carried instruments of measurement, journals, or maps.

- His clothing might reflect functionality over military form—breeches, boots, wool coat.

- He may have formed bonds with other settlers like Captain Grass, helping establish the foundation of Loyalist Kingston.

Let him walk your pages as one of the quiet architects of a new world, and through fiction, let his legacy unfold.

www.wikitree.com/wiki/McLean-13973[1]

Robert Denike

Born c. 1750s – Died after 1804

---

1.   http://www.wikitree.com/wiki/McLean-13973

Kingston Township settler, landholder, Loyalist

Scene: Autumn 1783 – New York, just before the Loyalist departure

The morning light filtered through the weather-stained shutters of the Denike home as Robert stood silently at the edge of the yard, the fresh news still hanging in the air like the season's last breath: the war was over.

It should have brought relief. Peace at last. But Robert Denike's jaw was tight. His hands, rough from labour, were clasped behind his back as he watched the road—a road he'd soon leave behind.

"They've signed it," came the voice of his friend, the messenger who had brought word. "The Treaty. It's official. We lost."

Robert gave a single nod. Not in resignation, but recognition. The American cause had prevailed. He was now a stranger in the land of his birth.

"We'll follow Grass," he said finally. "Cataraqui. That's where we'll make a future. There's no home left for us here."

He spoke with certainty, not bravado. Denike was a man of grounded realism, and though he had not been a soldier, he had been loyal—to Crown, to kin, and to the Loyalist cause. That loyalty now meant exile. But it also meant beginning again.

He turned to his wife, who stood at the doorway with a bundle of papers: land petitions, letters, a page listing settlers, his own name scrawled next to that of men he trusted—Robins, McLean, Graham... and Captain Grass himself.

"We go north," he said. "And we start fresh."

It would not be easy. But as Robert Denike looked once more at the horizon, his gaze held something steady and enduring. This was not an end—it was the beginning of Upper Canada.

Author's Section: Writing Robert Denike into Fiction

Robert Denike represents the quiet backbone of Loyalist resettlement: not a commanding officer or famed figure, but a steadfast settler whose name appears in early Kingston records beside men like Capt. Grass, William Robins, and Allan McLean. These were not simply farmers—they were the founders of a new society built from loss.

Writing Tips:

Denike's character can anchor your story in the civilian Loyalist experience. He likely wasn't a career soldier, but someone who believed deeply in the Crown and the order it represented. His loyalty came at great personal cost.

Explore his relationship to the land: the idea of being dispossessed in New York and beginning again in the wilds of Upper Canada. His resilience would've been tempered by heartbreak.

His practical nature makes him an excellent foil for more fiery characters. He may not give grand speeches, but his word carries weight.

Use his association with others—Grass, Robins, Graham—as a way to show how communities formed organically in exile, with friendships forged through shared ordeal.

HISTORICAL DETAILS to Consider:

Like many Loyalists, Denike likely traveled light, with only what his family could carry. His land record for Lot 2, Concession 16 suggests he eventually succeeded in establishing roots.

He may have kept or carried documents—grants, Crown papers, or proof of Loyalist service—essential for land claims.

His dress would have been modest: coarse woolen breeches, linen shirt, leather shoes worn thin from walking north.

By weaving Robert Denike into your story, you honour one of the many unsung founders whose quiet strength helped shape the land beneath Kingston's stones. In your hands, he walks again—one step closer to being remembered.

www.wikitree.com/wiki/Denike-71[2]

---

2.   http://www.wikitree.com/wiki/Denike-71

Godline Mop

Character Scene: The Birth of Godline Mop
Cataraqui (Kingston), Upper Canada – Autumn 1783

The air was thick with woodsmoke and the sharp, clean scent of wet cedar. The baby came just after sundown, while the wind was lifting the canvas edges of the makeshift tent that passed for shelter. No midwife, only hands worn raw from the war—another Loyalist woman who had delivered enough children to trust in instinct over elegance.

They wrapped the boy in what they had—a coarse linen shift and a square of Hudson's Bay wool too valuable to waste. Outside, the settlement was still a clutch of wagons, axes, and silent prayers. Inside, the boy's first cry pierced the hush, answered by a raven calling from the pine ridge overhead.

"Godline," the mother whispered, breathless, blinking against tears and exhaustion. No record survives to tell us who she was—only that she gave her son a name more holy than grand, a name that would echo through fields and deeds long after her own vanished.

The campfire crackled beside her as she held her infant close, uncertain whether the morning would bring warmth or frost. What she did know was this: he was born free. Not in rebellion, not in retreat, but in the stubborn soil of a new beginning. Godline Mop would not remember that night, but it would remember him.

AUTHOR'S SECTION: WRITING Godline Mop into Fiction

Godline Mop is one of those rare names in early Canadian history that seems drawn from scripture, soil, and myth. Born in 1783, the year the American Revolution ended and the Loyalist resettlement began, his very existence marks him as a child of the exodus. He lived an astonishing 99 years, dying in Walsingham Township in 1882 of "retinal decay," a poetic term for a long, slow fading of sight—perhaps symbolic for a man who had seen so much.

Writing Tips:

Frame Godline as a child of hardship and resilience. His unknown parentage makes him a blank slate, perfect for fictional elaboration.

Consider his name—Godline—and what it meant to the family who gave it. Religious? Symbolic? A tribute to survival?

He would've grown up amid Kingston's transformation from wilderness camp to garrison town. Write scenes from a child's perspective watching trees fall, roads form, soldiers march.

As a farmer, he would be deeply rooted in the land. Show him growing older with the colony itself.

Explore how someone born to a forgotten parent in a struggling encampment could live to nearly see Confederation.

WITH YOUR PEN, YOU return flesh to name, breath to record. Godline Mop's life is no longer a footnote—it's a story waiting to be told.

www.wikitree.com/wiki/Mop-2[1]

---

1.   http://www.wikitree.com/wiki/Mop-2

Mr. Sweeney

Character Scene: Mr. Sweeney Reacts to the End of the War
Cataraqui (Kingston), Upper Canada – Autumn 1783

Mr. Sweeney stood ankle-deep in the dark, stubborn mud that passed for a road, a cedar fence half-built behind him, and a battered satchel of nails slung over one shoulder. The news had come by word of mouth, carried on the same breath as the wind off Lake Ontario: *The war is over.*

He said nothing at first. Just squinted up at the gray sky as if it might split open with some heavenly confirmation. His hands, callused and cracked, closed around the handle of his hammer like it might vanish otherwise.

He'd built more than fences here—he'd built his second life. The first had been left behind when he and his kin had pledged loyalty to a crown that now sat distant and tarnished. His home in the old colonies was gone. His neighbours had taken up arms against him. And for years, he had survived on rations, bitterness, and the sheer weight of stubbornness.

Now, at last, peace.

"It's finished, then," he muttered to no one in particular, though a nearby boy paused with a pail in hand to listen. "And we're still standing."

He looked over the land. The stumps that needed clearing. The rude huts hammered together in defiance of despair. The new church bell still in its crate. All of it waiting.

Mr. Sweeney wasn't the type to weep, but he felt a tightness in his throat. He spat into the mud, rolled up his sleeves, and said, "Then it's time we build something worth the cost."

Author's Section: Writing Mr. Sweeney into Fiction

Mr. Sweeney represents the average but irreplaceable Loyalist settler—gritty, practical, and often unnamed in the grand sweep of history. His life speaks to the thousands of families and individuals who lost everything and chose to rebuild, not out of hope alone, but because they had no other choice.

Writing Tips:

• Give Mr. Sweeney the weight of a working man—hands that know tools, a body used to hardship. His reaction to peace won't be grand speeches, but small acts of resolve.

• His background can be Irish, Scottish, or English—perhaps a tenant farmer or tradesman who sided with the British Crown in the hopes of land and stability.

• Let his voice be sharp, dry, and a touch cynical—but not bitter. He's the type who survives because he can laugh at misery.

• He may not see himself as a leader, but others would trust him—especially in a settlement trying to define itself after war.

Whether he is a father, a neighbour, or a quiet pillar of his community, Mr. Sweeney's journey is one that should not be forgotten. He reminds us that history isn't only shaped by commanders and kings, but by men who keep hammering fence posts into frozen ground, even after peace is declared.

www.wikitree.com/wiki/Sweeney-4969[1]

1.   http://www.wikitree.com/wiki/Sweeney-4969

Thomas Cook

S cene: Late Autumn, 1783 – The News Reaches Thomas Cook
The trees were mostly bare now, their last leaves curling like old parchment, tossed by the wind that rolled off Lake Ontario. Thomas Cook stood at the edge of a clearing, his callused hand resting on the handle of the cart he'd pulled half the day. Behind him, a crude shelter made of cedar poles and sailcloth held his wife and children. They had made it this far north with what little they could carry—and even less certainty about what waited at the end.

He heard the news from a passing officer—mud-caked, grinning, mounted on a horse too fine for this trail.

"The war's done," the man shouted, tipping his hat. "Signed and sealed. Peace with the Americans."

Thomas didn't answer at first. He simply turned to look east, toward the tangled forests of the old colonies—his past now. New York, home once. Gone. His land, his neighbors, his kin who chose the rebel cause. Gone, too.

He took off his hat slowly, pressing the brim to his chest.

"Done, is it?" he murmured, voice low so only the trees heard. "So be it."

His eldest boy, no more than twelve, came to stand beside him.

"Does that mean we can go home?" the boy asked.

Thomas shook his head, gently. "No, lad. This is home now."

And with that, he bent to the cart once more and hauled it up the rough trail—toward the future, toward Cataraqui.

AUTHOR'S SECTION: WRITING Thomas Cook Into Fiction

Thomas Cook is a Loyalist settler of sparse record but deep potential. His land grant in 1787 confirms his loyalty to the Crown, his family's presence in early Kingston, and his endurance through the turbulent resettlement years. We know his name, his reward, and the oath he swore to a new land. The rest is yours to imagine.

Writing Tips:

Thomas is a survivor, not a soldier. There are no records of his military service, which suggests he may have been a civilian Loyalist—perhaps a tradesman, tenant farmer, or even a tavern keeper who paid dearly for his allegiance.

The war's end is bittersweet. He has endured exile, hardship, and silence from loved ones left behind. Peace may bring rest, but not restoration.

Make him practical. He's not a man for speeches. His loyalty is quiet, measured in the swing of his axe and the calloused skin of his hands.

CHARACTER TRAITS TO Explore:

Stubborn and principled: He didn't bend when others did.

Protective father: His motivation is survival for his family.

Haunted by the past: Every shovel of new earth reminds him what he lost.

Skeptical but determined: He trusts land and labor more than politics now.

HISTORICAL ANCHORS:

Land grant dated October 22, 1787 places him in Kingston Township, Lot 7, Concession 5.

Seigneurie of N. likely refers to the French seigneurial system still in use in parts of the province—Thomas is stepping into an unfamiliar legal landscape.

Oaths taken and a promise of a patent point to his full compliance with British settlement policy.

A later mortgage involving his lot in 1812 suggests his land endured, even if Thomas himself did not.

THEMES TO EXPLORE:

Loyalty without reward: Not all Loyalists were welcomed equally. Thomas may feel overlooked or forgotten.

The cost of silence: He doesn't speak of the war—not to his wife, not to his children—but it shows in the way he listens to the wind.

Rebuilding and legacy: His work is not for himself, but for those who'll come after. He is the first stone in a future town.

SYMBOLIC MOTIFS:

An empty homestead key: Carried from New York, now useless.

A weathered family Bible: Pages worn, but names still written in.

The land patent: Promised, not yet delivered. It represents hope, uncertainty, and permanence all at once.

LEGACY: THOMAS COOK is one of Kingston's invisible founders. His bones may rest quietly beneath modern pavement, but the land remembers him. When writers bring him to life, they bring voice to

thousands of Loyalist settlers who swore the oath, tilled the frost-hardened soil, and built a future on land they had to learn to love.
www.wikitree.com/wiki/Cook-57035[1]

---

1.   http://www.wikitree.com/wiki/Cook-57035

Thomas Markland

S cene: Thomas Markland's Reaction to the End of the American Revolution

The year was 1783, and the wind off Lake Ontario carried a bitter chill as Thomas Markland sat in his study, the heavy weight of the evening's news settling in his chest. The report had come to him through an acquaintance—a local merchant who had heard the official word: the American Revolution had ended. The treaty had been signed. The colonies had secured their independence.

He placed his quill down slowly, his hand trembling ever so slightly. The flames from the hearth flickered and cast long shadows across the room, but the warmth of the fire did little to thaw the coldness creeping into his bones. Outside, the world was changing, and for men like him, it felt as though the earth itself was shifting beneath his feet.

Thomas had long believed in the British cause, holding steadfast to the Crown's authority even as the colonies spiraled toward rebellion. But now, as he sat there, the weight of defeat pressed on him. His loyalty to Britain had once felt like a badge of honor, but now, with the ink drying on the treaty that marked Britain's loss, he was left to wonder what would become of his family's future.

The estate—his land, his home—had always been tied to his allegiance. If the Americans were now in charge of these lands, what would become of men like him? Those who had fought for the British cause, those who had been loyal to the Crown—how would they be treated now that peace had been made?

He stood abruptly, walking to the window and staring out into the darkness at the quiet streets bathed in the soft glow of candlelight from the homes of his neighbors. How many of them had fought for the rebels? How many would now look at him with suspicion, perhaps even disdain, for his loyalty to the Crown?

The war had been long and costly, not just in lives but in friendships and allegiances. There were families torn apart by conflicting loyalties—brothers against brothers, fathers against sons. And now, with the war officially over, what was left for men like Thomas? He had remained neutral in many respects, unwilling to raise arms himself, but his heart had always been with Britain. And yet, in the eyes of the new American republic, how would he be seen?

A knock at the door broke his reverie, and Thomas turned to face the entrance. It was his son, no doubt with news of his own—of how the war's end had been received in other parts of the town.

"Father," his son said, stepping into the room, his voice uncertain. "I heard the news. It's over. The treaty... the colonies are free."

Thomas nodded, his lips tight as he met his son's gaze. "Yes, it's over. And now we face what comes next."

His son waited, as if expecting more, but Thomas had no words. His heart was heavy with the knowledge that his world had changed, and there was no going back. The American Revolution had ended, but for men like him, it was only the beginning of a new, uncertain chapter.

"There's nothing more to be done now," Thomas said finally, his voice steady but distant. "Only wait and see what becomes of us."

As his son left the room, Thomas Markland remained by the window, staring out into the night. The storm had passed, but the aftermath would leave scars that would take years to heal.

The Crown had lost, and Thomas Markland wondered how long it would take for him to lose everything else.

AUTHOR INSPIRATION: Thomas Markland

Full Name: Thomas Markland

Birth Year: Likely early 1700s

Death Year: Prior to 1812 (as evidenced by his absence in the 1812 mortgage transaction).

Location: Kingston, Ontario (Province of Quebec at the time)

OCCUPATION AND SOCIAL Standing:

Thomas Markland was a prominent landowner in Kingston, situated in the 5th Concession. His title as "Esquire" denotes a man of some standing, likely an educated, well-regarded member of the community. He would have been well-versed in managing land, overseeing his estate, and engaging in the governance of the region.

He owned land that would later pass to his heirs, his role as "heir at law" reflecting a connection to a family legacy. His involvement in property transactions—such as the sale of land to John Cartwright—shows his active participation in the legal and business affairs of the time. The way he held his land and wealth suggests a man deeply invested in securing his family's future and maintaining his place in society.

PERSONALITY:

Thomas Markland would have carried himself with a sense of quiet duty. His life revolved around ensuring that his land was maintained, his family prospered, and his legacy endured. He was pragmatic, perhaps reserved, and deeply loyal to the Crown. His loyalty to Britain, even after the Revolution, would have shaped how he viewed the world, particularly now that the colonies had gained independence.

Though not necessarily a soldier in the conflict, he would have supported the British cause in ways that mattered: through financial backing, moral support, and even enduring the social and political ramifications of living in a land divided by rebellion. A stoic and private man, Thomas likely kept his emotions in check, hiding his personal disappointment or bitterness over the defeat of the Crown. His world was changing, and the transition from a loyal subject of the Crown to something uncertain would have been a heavy burden for a man like him.

FAMILY:

As an heir, Thomas Markland was part of a long family legacy, and this would have weighed heavily on his shoulders. He would have seen it as his duty to carry on that legacy and secure his family's position. His connections to the land were more than just about wealth—they were about heritage. Any shift in ownership or power would have threatened that legacy.

Given his stature, he likely had children who would inherit his estate and carry the Markland name forward. The thought of his descendants living under a new government, possibly hostile to his Loyalist background, may have weighed on him heavily. The future of his family and their land was tied to the survival of the old order—and that survival was now in question.

WHAT HE WORE:

Thomas Markland, as an Esquire, would have dressed in the formal manner typical for someone of his social standing. Picture him in a well-fitted, dark woolen coat, its tailored cut fitting closely around his shoulders, buttoned high with brass buttons that gleamed faintly in the candlelight of his study. His waistcoat beneath would have been of a rich fabric, perhaps a dark silk or velvet, embroidered at the edges with subtle designs—reflecting both his status and his wealth.

His breeches would have been of a matching dark fabric, tucked neatly into high black leather boots, polished to a shine, though scuffed slightly from his work around the estate. His cravat would be tightly tied, and a stiff, white shirt would show beneath, its high collar sharp and unyielding—a symbol of his serious and reserved nature.

In quieter moments, Thomas may have worn a simple, but well-crafted brown or black overcoat when venturing outside, the broad lapels and deep pockets practical for carrying letters and small papers. A tri-corner hat would have been a familiar part of his attire, worn when meeting with local officials or managing business dealings.

His overall appearance would have been impeccable, but not in an ostentatious way; he was a man who dressed to convey authority and respect, rather than for show.

www.wikitree.com/wiki/Markland-476[1]

---

1.   http://www.wikitree.com/wiki/Markland-476

Don't miss out!

Visit the website below and you can sign up to receive emails whenever Angeline Gallant publishes a new book. There's no charge and no obligation.

https://books2read.com/r/B-A-QGSI-ZQUZB

BOOKS2READ

Connecting independent readers to independent writers.

Also by Angeline Gallant

A Dragon's Diary
Dreaming of Dragons

Blood and Spirit Saga
The Rising Wind
Fate's Promise

Calling Her Heart
Whisper of the Heart
Calling Her Heart Boxed Set Volumes 1-4
Calling Her Heart Volumes 1 & 2: A Small Town Romance
Collection
No Turning Back
Calling Her Heart volumes 3 & 4
Forsake Me Not
Hear My Cry

FORGET ME NOT

Victoria, Ontario's Babies 1894 - 1895

GENERATIONS OF THE VOLGA
A Family's Legacy

Guardian of the Heart
Fallen Petals

Keeper Of Secrets
A Lady's Secret

Kingston's Love Chronicles
Springtime Promises

Midnight's Awakening
Heart of the Storm
Walking Through The Storm
Walking Through The Storm
Fighting the Storm
Call Me Cursed
Heart of the Storm

Secrets of the Underworld

Deklan's Dragons

Tell My Story Collection
Tell My Story: Germany 1851
Tell My Story: England 1852
Whispers From The Garrison Church
Loyalist Echoes of 1783

The Dervock Legacy
Echoes of Dervock

The Grave Whisperer
German Prisoners of War in Canada
Cataraqui United Church Cemetery
Whispers of Kingston
Wedding Bells in Kingston, Ontario, Canada 1923
St. Paul's Anglican Churchyard A-B
St. Paul's Anglican Churchyard C-D
St. Paul's Anglican Churchyard E - F
St. Paul's Anglican Churchyard G - H
St. Paul's Anglican Churchyard J - N
St. Paul's Anglican Churchyard O - R
St. Paul's Anglican Churchyard S - T
St. Paul's Anglican Churchyard, Kingston, Ontario T - Z
Small Graveyards & Burial Grounds: Kingston, Ontario, Canada
Cataraqui United Church Cemetery 1
Cataraqui United Church Cemetery 2
Cataraqui United Church Cemetary 3

Cataraqui United Church Cemetery 4
Cataraqui United Church Cemetery 5
Beth Israel Cemetery
Cataraqui United Church Cemetery 6
Beneath the Surface: Echoes from Beth Israel Cemetery
Grave Tales: Discovering the Lives of Beth Israel
Whispers Beneath St. Paul's
Unveiled

The Timeless Veil
Eternal Devotion

The Wolf Whisperer Series
The Cry of the Wolf
Journey of the Heart
Captured Heart
Fate's Legacy
Mohawk Valley
Cry of a Warrior
Wolf Whisperer volumes 1 & 2
Endless White
The Wolf Whisperer Volumes 1-4
The Wolf Whisperer volumes 1 & 2

Timeless
The Time Keeper's Sanctuary
Timeless Souls

Timeless Echoes
Timeless Roots
Echoes of Storrington
Timeless Echoes
Buried Beneath
Echoes of Kingston
Tracing Kingston's Past

Timeless Whispers of Dervock Saga
Secrets of Dervock

Standalone
Winds of Change vol 1-3

Watch for more at https://www.goodreads.com/author/show/19703964.Angeline_Gallant.

About the Author

Angeline Gallant traces her roots through generations of Old Stock Canadian heritage, her passion for genealogy as deep and enduring as the forests and fields her ancestors once walked. With a reverence for history and an eye for detail, she weaves stories from the fragments of lives left behind in letters, records, and weathered headstones.

An avid reader and devoted writer, Angeline brings the past to life with a curiosity for heraldry and a deep love for the landscapes that shaped her family's story. Each name and date she uncovers feels less like history and more like coming home, a familiar echo in the vast tapestry of time. For her, these stories are not forgotten—they live, breathing in the quiet spaces of memory and tradition, a testament to lives once lived, now eternal in the pages of her books.

Read more at https://www.goodreads.com/author/show/ 19703964.Angeline_Gallant.